'Tween Crayons and Curfews

Tips for Middle School Teachers

Heather Wolpert-Gawron
aka Tweenteacher

EYE ON EDUCATION
6 DEPOT WAY WEST, SUITE 106
LARCHMONT, NY 10538
(914) 833–0551
(914) 833–0761 fax
www.eyeoneducation.com

Library of Congress Cataloging-in-Publication Data

Wolpert-Gawron, Heather.
  'Tween crayons and curfews : tips for middle school teachers / by Heather Wolpert-Gawron.
    p. cm.
  ISBN 978-1-59667-180-5
  1. Middle school teachers—United States—Handbooks, manuals, etc. 2. Middle school teaching—United States—Handbooks, manuals, etc. 3. Middle schools—United States—Handbooks, manuals, etc. 4. Preteens—Education (Middle school)—United States. 5. Preteens—United States—Attitudes. 6. Preteens—United States—Social life and customs. I. Title.

  LB1776.5.W65 2011

  373.236—dc22

                                                    2011000042

10 9 8 7 6 5 4 3 2

Also Available from EYE ON EDUCATION

The Passion-Driven Classroom:
A Framework for Teaching and Learning
Angela Maiers and Amy Sandvold

Helping Students Motivate Themselves:
Practical Answers to Classroom Challenges
Larry Ferlazzo

Rigor is NOT a Four-Letter Word
Barbara R. Blackburn

Classroom Motivation from A to Z:
How to Engage Your Students in Learning
Barbara R. Blackburn

Battling Boredom: 99 Strategies to Spark Student Engagement
Bryan Harris

50 Ways to Improve Student Behavior:
Simple Solutions to Complex Challenges
Annette Breaux and Todd Whitaker

101 Answers for New Teachers and Their Mentors:
Effective Teaching Tips for Daily Classroom Use
Annette L. Breaux

How the Best Teachers Avoid the 20 Most Common Teaching Mistakes
Elizabeth Breaux

Formative Assessment for English Language Arts:
A Guide for Middle and High School Teachers
Amy Benjamin

Teaching, Learning, and Assessment Together:
Reflective Assessments
Arthur K. Ellis

What Do You Say When…?
Best Practice Language for Improving Student Behavior
Hal Holloman and Peggy H. Yates

ENGAGING Teens in Their Own Learning:
8 Keys to Student Success
Paul Vermette

Foreword

I first met Heather Wolpert-Gawron in the winter of 2008 at a meeting of Edutopia bloggers at our offices next to Skywalker Ranch. Our staff had sought their advice on future directions in education and how Edutopia media and our community of bloggers might support teachers in moving towards that future. Heather's participation in the meeting mirrored her wonderful blogs, combining boundless enthusiasm, great ideas, and a multifaceted and farsighted vision of teaching with technology, all rooted in her experience as a middle school teacher.

Middle school students, no longer young children and developing into teenagers, need a certain special kind of teacher. Heather epitomizes this teacher who thrives on teaching "tweeners." In *'Tween Crayons and Curfews: Tips for Middle School Teachers*, Heather dives into the "tween" brain and emerges with the "tween" heart. She was compelled to write this book to fuel a middle school teachers' movement based on the pride and enjoyment of working with this energetic and ever-changing group of students.

Heather's lessons and writing call to middle schoolers and the teachers who are called to teach them. Her keen understanding of how middle school students think and behave is apparent on every page. She has also scaffolded her methods so that teachers at all grade levels can learn and adapt the strategies she's researched, developed, and perfected.

Heather is also a teaching realist. She knows that teaching is hard and doesn't pretend that her concepts and lessons are silver bullets for the challenges teachers face every day. But she is a bulldog in her stubbornness that the difficulties of teaching need not lead to despair. In fact, her advice boils down to one single point: what makes a happy teacher also makes for happier students, and happier students achieve more deeply. Her advice is meant to make the job easier and the teacher more fulfilled. As a result, students exceed expectations.

While many education books are published each year by researchers, policy analysts, and futurists, those written by teachers speak with a distinctive and instantly recognizable voice. Their voices are closest to the students and, ultimately, the voices of teachers and students are the most important. Inside this book is the voice of that talented teacher I heard at our meeting several years ago. Heather Wolpert-Gawron was a joy to listen to then and this book brings you the joy of listening to her now.

Milton Chen, Ph.D.
Senior Fellow & Executive Director, Emeritus
The George Lucas Educational Foundation
Edutopia.org

Acknowledgements

I have been blessed to have and work with some great teachers in my lifetime and, as a teacher I find myself referencing their style and influence in my own practice. There was Ms. Lydon, who helped a disinterested kid link to learning by recognizing in me a talent not tested on a bubble exam. There was Ms. Sauve, who always found the humor in every transition and allowed student choice in any project, drawing out the best of us. There was Ms. Wallace, who knew that a great discussion in class could not be hampered by a silly rule like, "You must sit at your desk." Rather, those of us lucky enough to participate in her dynamic discussions were driven to sit on their desks, our excitement pulling us from our polite places of static learning.

I have also been influenced by teachers I have worked with in every school throughout my career. There was Suky Werman, my coteacher for the first two years of my teaching career. She put up with my wild ideas, refined them, and introduced me to her passion for curriculum integration as a means to make things exciting for her students and for herself. There was Addie Holsing, my first teacher mentor in the public schools, who took me under her wing when the frustrations of teaching in an inner city school were almost too great for a newer teacher to bear without a veteran's direction. Her friendship and wisdom helped hone my classroom structure to reflect a student's brain development. There was Elaine Keysor, who became a daily source of friendship and collaboration, both personally and professionally. Each day after school, we would don our walking shoes and go for a stroll, sharing our struggles and advising each other on solutions, dreaming of directions to take our classes. Every day with her was a battery-charging experience for the brain, and not a day goes by that I do not miss her by my side.

Even now, I am surrounded by teachers who influence me and help guide my practice. There are my fellows of the UCI Writing Project, led by Carol Booth Olson and Catherine D'Aoust. There's my daily lunch crew: Liz Harrington, Suzie Menerey, and Darlene Pope, who are each fearless in curriculum experimentation and collaboration, and, despite their many years in the classroom, continue to refine and redesign lessons to keep things new and applicable for their students. There's Jackie Avakian, who tolerates my questions about technology, answering every one of them to help me be able to dream bigger the next time. There's Kenna McRae, who, through the use of props and kinesthetic strategies, lures her students to deeper learning. She has a gift for challenging those struggling students in such a way that by the end of the year, they begin to ask more of themselves than even she asks of them. There's Betsy "Alice" Huff, who developed an art elective as rigorous as any advanced calculus class. In our education policy debates, I continue to learn from her with every discussion. I am in awe of her dedication to the ideal educational world, and if she ever started a school, I'd be the first teacher to sign up.

Beyond the scope of teachers, I have been blessed to work with face-to-face with those who have become my online colleagues and friends. There are the crew members that make up the Center for Teaching Quality, who constantly give me a shot of brain adrenalin with their discussions about educational policy and pedagogy. And special thanks must go out to John Norton, a gifted online moderator and the dearest cheerleader any teacher or blogger could have standing behind her. There's also the staff and educators of The George Lucas Educational Foundation and Edutopia.org, who make me proud everyday to be on their team.

But as influential as teachers are inside education, great teachers also come from outside the school world. First of all, I want to thank my sister, who has always been there with megaphone in hand, rooting for me, and who once reminded me that to really achieve in life, we all have to invest in our abilities and ourselves. Without that reminder, I would not have set into place the building blocks that were to become this very book.

I want to thank my parents for being my first and best teachers, and for setting a high expectation for all instructors to come. Every moment in my home was a learning one, full of storytelling and dialogue, full of challenges and solutions. Our home was known as "The Hubbubery" because of the passionate buzz of conversation, laughter, tears, questioning, answering, and praise that blessed each of our rooms and surrounded anyone who entered through its doors.

Which brings me to the man who helped me establish my own home that continued that tradition of warmth, support, and discourse: my husband Royce. It is he who taught me a greater ease in using technology to allow my own stories to be told and lessons to be shared. When I started blogging and writing, ours became a surprise partnership for both of us, as he helped me through the how, allowing me to focus on the what. To this day, when I come home with some crazy idea, he's immediately onboard and ready to help me figure it out. Without him, I would not currently have a stake in the future of education, a passion for the world of educational technology. His ability and flexibility have allowed me to dream and follow through with those dreams.

Lastly, I would like to thank my son Benjamin. Even as I write this, he's too young to know how he has influenced me as a teacher, but he is the one who first made me a parent, the most important teacher of all.

Meet the Author

Heather Wolpert-Gawron is an award-winning middle school teacher who also writes a popular education blog known as Tweenteacher. She has authored workbooks on teaching Internet Literacy for grades 3 to 8 and is currently working on another set of workbooks on writing the Multi-Genre Research Report for Teacher-Created Resources. Heather also blogs for The George Lucas Educational Foundation's Edutopia.org and moderates their middle school discussion group. Additionally, she has joined the educational blogger staff at The Huffington Post. She is a member of the Center for Teaching Quality's Teacher Leaders Network, a Fellow of the National Writing Project, and is devoted to helping teachers regain control of their profession through elevating their practice and educating themselves on policy. She is married to Royce, whom she met in second grade after karate-chopping him at recess. Additionally, she is mom to her crazy-wonderful four-year-old son, Benjamin, who will begin public school in the fall of 2011. At the time of this book's publication, she is awaiting the birth of her second son, whose name she cannot disclose as she has been sworn to secrecy prior to his birth. She lives with all her boys, their boxer/corgi mix, and their laughter and chaos in Los Angeles, CA.

Free Downloads

Some of the tools discussed and displayed in this book are also available on Eye On Education's website as Adobe Acrobat files. Permission has been granted to purchasers of this book to download these tools and print them.

You can access these downloads by visiting Eye On Education's website: www.eyeoneducation.com. Click FREE Downloads or search or browse our website to find this book and then scroll down for downloading instructions.

You'll need your book buyer access code: **TCC-7180-5**

Index of Downloads

Contents

Introduction

Teaching tweens is a calling that requires a very particular teacher. A superteacher. A tween teacher. Tweens and teens, after all, can be energy succubae, draining a teacher's drive with their developmental bifurcation, decibels, and drama. Therefore, as teachers of the middle children of education, you have to develop very specific tools to reach them.

The book that you now hold in your hands will help you achieve two goals. It will give you strategies to help you be a better teacher in the tween classroom, guiding your students from middle schoolers to middle scholars. It also will help you find that necessary happiness in this difficult job of ours, because your own happiness as a teacher trickles down to greater happiness in your students, and their comfort in your classroom boils down to greater achievement.

Let me repeat that: if you're happy, everything else is going to fall into place. Happiness is your silver bullet to easier classroom management and greater student achievement. It's that simple.

'Tween Crayons and Curfews: Tips for Middle School Teachers discusses proven ways to engage students, teach with rigor, and be a collaborator in student achievement. It combines theory with the immediate next-day lessons and step-by-step guides that are meant to make a difficult job easier, and a hard job more enjoyable.

Because teaching can be hard. Really hard. We all know this job is fraught with challenges we never signed up for, and we're held accountable for failings we have no control over. However, if you don't figure out how to love teaching, with all of its obstacles and insults, then your students will not love learning.

Unhappy teacher = unhappy student = low achievement = unhappier teacher

Frankly, it doesn't matter if you're a new teacher, fresh off the credential program, a Teach for America intern struggling through your committed time, a veteran ready to throw in the towel, or a second-career teacher having leapt onto our educational ladder, this book can help you cut the corners of confusion, giving you strategies to help you navigate through this difficult yet rewarding career.

As a classroom teacher in the middle school, I am constantly in the field with the lessons and activities that you will read about here. I am constantly tweaking and refining, throwing out what doesn't work, and bronzing for all eternity that which does. My work is a work in progress, just as middle schoolers are all works in progress.

In this book I share what works for me, what keeps me happy, what keeps me wanting to work hard, and what keeps me the level of teacher that I can be proud of. It all translates to the success of my students; and let's face it—their success, their true success, as lifelong learners and people who intrinsically want to succeed, helps me achieve my own happiness. I'm selfish that way. I'm not interested in being miserable and spending my day unhappy. Call me crazy.

Of course I'm crazy. I love teaching tweens.

What is a Tween?

Let's do a little analogy. Please think about the stages of metamorphosis when answering:

Elementary students are to caterpillars as high schoolers are to butterflies.

Therefore, high schoolers are to butterflies as middle school students are to _____.

Answer: Howler monkeys. That's right. Somewhere between caterpillars and butterflies, the human child becomes an entirely different species. OK, maybe they are not totally unrecognizable, but the fact is that tweens straddle two worlds, and that defines a lot of who they are during this time of their life and how they function as learners.

In any tween classroom, let's say from around fifth grade to ninth grade, you have students who watch CNN and those who still watch the Disney Channel. There are kids "playing doctor," and those still playing patty cake. There are kids who have their eyes set on the high school college entrance requirements, and those who still need to be watched to make sure they put their homework in their backpack.

At times, seeing the diversity in my own students, I've wondered who I was when I was in middle school.

I believe it's important to have transparency in a school. In fact, I'm kind of an open book with my colleagues. I willingly confess my test scores, my flops, my challenges, and I'm not embarrassed by my victories. Frankly, my department probably knows more about my foibles then my own husband. OK, that's an exaggeration, but you get the drift.

In the spirit of transparency, because we're talking about teaching middle schoolers, I wanted to begin this educational journey by introducing you to me, when I was a tween. As a result, I've developed my Top 10 List of Memories from Middle School. I provide this list to make a point. After all, when we become adults, we tend to forget what really drives a tween's train, and it's very valuable as an educator to reflect back on whom you were when you were in school at that time of your life.

Try developing your own list sometime. Need help jarring your memory? See my list of questions at the end of this introduction. Because the fact is that by remembering what had the greatest impact on you when you were a student, you can become a better teacher.

Ladies and gentlemen, fellow teachers. Here is Heather Wolpert-Gawron, the middle schooler:

1. **Zits.** I remember waking up to find what I was sure to be the mother of all zits taking up residence on my cheek. I tried everything to hide it. I ended up putting gobs of blush on my left check, trying to balance the red on the right one. As a result, my counselor pulled me into her office and asked, "Heather, honey? Are your parents treating you alright?" The abused child look. Not what I was going for. Sometimes you look better than you think you do. Sometimes you look worse.

2. **Laughing.** I don't remember what the boy whispered next to me. Looking back, I'm sure it was not that funny. But I remember laughing so hard during Mr. Canon's English class that I literally shot the grape I had been eating out my nose at the person's head in front of me, eliciting an "ow!" from the student and a threatened detention from Mr. Canon. I talked my teacher out of giving me detention, explaining that laughing was a natural reaction to a humorous quip. I learned that I could talk a teacher out of anything so long as the debate took place at the end of the period before lunch.

3. **Boys.** Sean, Pete, David, Mario. All of them crossed my mind one time or another. Notice, however, I didn't mention the quiet, football-playing, *Dungeons and Dragons* guy in the corner who, incidentally, I ended up marrying in 2002. Clearly we can't bank on knowing how our tween students will turn out based on who they are in middle school. Academically, socially…they aren't a closed book already.

4. **Friends.** Megan, Kristy, Shami, Caroline, Melissa, Beth, the list goes on. Some of them I didn't even get along with so well, but I still considered them friends. Tweens aren't known for being too picky.

5. **Fashion.** I was in middle school when Cindi Lauper and Madonna both burst onto the scene in their bustiers, toile skirts, and rubber bracelets. My parents wouldn't let me have the black

rubber bracelets everyone was wearing, calling them "trashy." But Beth let me borrow up to 10 of them per day from her wrist-to-elbow stock. She was like a fashionista librarian, requiring formal checkout procedures if you were going to borrow her bracelets. Looking back, my parents were probably onto something.

6. **All The Right Moves.** *All the Right Moves* (1983) was an early Tom Cruise movie about a young man in high school who played football, trying to get out of his small town. Whatever. All I remember about *All The Right Moves* is glimpsing a certain part of the male anatomy on screen for the first time. My friend Beth rewound that tape so many times that even the 13-year-old girls at her sleepover got bored.

7. **An Unsupervised Party.** I was in eighth grade when I attended my first unsupervised party. I seem to remember being surprised upon my arrival to find that there was no adult supervision present. However, I was not so horrified that I called to be picked up again. It was there that I saw my first joint passed at a party. I turned it down, but I was the only kid who did. Everyone else at the party was from what you might call "the good kids" clique, according to adults. They were the A and B students, cheerleaders, football players, churchgoers, whatever. They were the winners of the citizenship awards, the penmanship awards, and the perfect attendance awards. One of the boys asked me if I wanted to have sex. I said, "no thanks." He rolled his eyes and asked if I was planning on holding out until marriage. It seemed to me, however, that there was a lot of time between eighth grade and marriage to make that decision. Passing on the dope probably knocked my popularity points down a notch; but passing on eighth grade sex probably saved my popularity points from plummeting.

8. **Family Differences.** I remember sitting on the curb at school, bored and waiting to be picked up by my carpool, when a mom pulled up to pick up her student. She drove up quickly, bumping up onto the curb near me, and stumbling, got out of her car. She was drunk. "Do you know where Tim is?" she slurred. I shrugged, yet knew exactly where her kid was. I just remembering wanting to buy some time. She stumbled off to look for herself, while I went running to a counselor to intercept the pickup. But by the time the adult and I got back to the place where the car had been parked, the kid had already been picked up and

the car was gone. It was one of the first times I remember thinking, "boy, have I got it good," understanding, really understanding, that many kids weren't lucky enough to have the home life that I did.

9. **Independent Monetary Decisions.** Middle school was when I first found myself able to make my own decisions about money and purchases, and it also happened to correspond to the explosive appearance of the local mall. At the mall, I could spend what little money I had on the latest Prince cassette or on a Hot-Dog-On-A-Stick with some friends. I was an independent gal on the town.

Now, so far, nowhere on this list do you see a mention of anything really school related, do you? Well, I do have one academic memory, coming in at number 10 on my hit list:

10. **My First A on a Paper.** In seventh grade I discovered adjectives. I confess that even though I had heard the word "adjectives" ever since third grade, it wasn't until seventh grade that I really understood what they meant and how to use them. I was writing an essay on ballooning and I wanted to describe the hot air balloon. I had this eureka moment, and I thought, "Hey, what about those adjective-things?" I got an A on the paper, but the feedback I received was the comment, "Too Descriptive." Sometimes teachers just don't recognize the true learning.

The point is that these memories could be the memories of any middle schooler even today (save for the Cindi Lauper reference.) In fact, if I'm really honest with myself, I have to admit that my tendencies as a teacher could very easily conflict with what's really important to a tween. I have to remind myself, that if I'm not careful, and if I don't very purposefully tap into what tweens naturally love, then my efforts may not rank as high as I would like them to on my students' own mythical lists.

Middle schoolers are unique because of their very placement in the academic timeline. They are so over the newness of school, which many elementary students still possess. Many are no longer still wide-eyed about school and recess and making the teacher happy. On the flip side, however, many don't yet have the imperativeness to achieve units or graduation requirements that can help motivate a high schooler. Now toss in hormones. That's our middle school clientele.

The Uniqueness of Teaching Tweens

So given that you are facing a classroom of students who probably don't even rank school as a huge priority and who arguably may not even be human, teaching such a diversity of learners, needless to say, takes specific skills. Therefore, if we really want to reach tweens in our teaching, we need to use certain strategies that exploit their tendencies. After all, just as we don't teach third graders like tenth graders, why wouldn't we tap into what makes tweens unique so as to teach them better?

Remember the howler monkeys? Well, much like monkeys, tweens also travel in groups, using hoots and hollers as a way to communicate love, hate, anger, and joy. We've all been in school assemblies filled with the sounds of the jungle, right? It's this very drive to constantly communicate, to constantly be social, that teachers must tap into if they are to be successful tween teachers. Typically, you see schools try to compete with tweens' tendencies to socialize, but rather, they should envelope it, harness it, and use it to help students achieve.

You can't insist on a well-behaved tween classroom. Or, that is, you can but you'll be fighting them all year long. Instead, we have to be strategic in our practice as middle school teachers. We have to set up lessons, procedures, and activities that tap into their interests. We have to build up our own tolerance to the general buzz of noise that accompanies any group of tweens and use it to our advantage. We have to appeal to the individuals in order to create a community of learners at an age when both being an individual and a community has its challenges.

For these reasons teaching tweens can be intimidating for many educators. In fact, in many districts, it's even harder to get a willing substitute teacher for middle school than for any other grade level. After all, tween teachers must be adept in elementary teaching practices like cooperative grouping and collaboration while also being experts in communicating content, at times at the high school level. For as unique as tweens are, they can also respond to both elementary strategies and high school-level ones. Your toolbox as a teacher should be packed with possibilities, and it's this need to use such a range in teaching strategies that makes teaching tweens so challenging. From the point of view of a true tween teacher, however, tapping into these challenges becomes an opportunity.

Your toolbox as a teacher should be packed with possibilities, and it's this need to use such a range in teaching strategies that makes teaching tweens so challenging.

When you seize those opportunities, and your students, in turn, have their own eureka moments, well, there's nothing else like it.

I'm a happy teacher. And it's certainly not because I don't see the problems in education or because I keep some eternal Pollyannaish smile on my face, but because I has found secret tips to avoid, leap, and dodge some of the day-to-day challenges of an otherwise difficult job.

I challenge you to not just do your job, but to love it. Happiness, is your silver bullet.

Welcome to my classroom, welcome to my practice, and welcome to my book.

Who Were You in Middle School?

The following questions will help to jar your memory and help you in your own middle school reflection. After all, in middle school, you're programmed to make mistakes and do things you regret; yet so many of us have blocked the memories out entirely. But by looking back at who you were, it helps to relate to those students you have now.

1. Did you have a nickname?

2. What were the names of your five closest friends? Did you even have friends?

3. How did you choose to spend your lunch or recess?

4. What music were you listening to?

5. Did you play a sport?

6. Were you involved in an after-school activity?

7. Had you already tried alcohol or drugs?

8. What was the name of the person or persons that you liked more than a friend?

9. What did you gossip about?

10. Did you ever pass notes in class?

11. Did you have a favorite teacher? What was his or her name? Why was that person your favorite?

12. Were you in a clique?

13. Were you a bully? A protector? A victim? A bystander?

14. How did you get to school?

15. What movies came out when you were in middle school?

16. Do you still own anything that you've kept since middle school?

17. Do you still have any friends you've had since middle school?

18. Did you have a favorite expression when you were in middle school?

19. Did you ever do something during those years that now makes you wince?

20. Is there a direct line between who you were then and who you are now, or are there only faint traces in that middle schooler to the person you've become?

Remember, who you were as a middle schooler may contribute to the person you are now, but it isn't set in stone. Keep in mind that middle schoolers are programmed to make mistakes and make bad decisions. A tween teacher helps students learn from the mistakes, shake off the guilt of having made them, and moves them ever closer to being the person they are meant to be.

1

Tips for Creating a Tween-Centric Classroom Environment

We have to recognize that human flourishing is not a mechanical process; it's an organic process....All you can do is, like a farmer, create the conditions under which they will begin to flourish.

— Sir Ken Robinson

Our budget's been slashed. We don't have funds for supplies. The bookcase behind your desk looks like the Leaning Tower of Pisa. Schools need furniture for every student and a workstation for each teacher with chairs that are balanced on all four legs. Schools need windows without webs of cracks, and faucets that run clean water. They need a little green, patches of landscaped carpet squares to lay on with a good book. The students need a tree to eat lunch under. Schools need to be freed of police tape, freed of asbestos, and freed of the landscape of concrete that makes learning feel more like a prison than a future.

Schools need to reflect a pride in the learning that occurs within. But regardless of what the school is doing to attain these goals, you still need to create an oasis in your classroom, within even the worst academic desert.

As a teacher, you are only in control of so much. Fortunately, your classroom, its appearance, setup, comfort, influence, and what happens between its four walls are important variables in education that you, the teacher, can do something about. It's all about making the decision that your classroom environment is important and making the most of what you have in order to address its appearance.

For students, their physical environment is vital in their level of engagement. After all, if teachers can't be troubled to create an environment of learning, then students are less likely to learn.

As we know, for tweens, appearance is everything. It's all about their hair, their clothes, and, yes, their classroom environment. Each day, tweens try on different costumes, striving for some sense of identity, but your classroom should know its place in the world, should be costumed in it, and should be comfortable in its own skin. Creating that confident environment creates a stable influence in the unstable life of the fluctuating tween.

> *If teachers can't be troubled to create an environment of learning, then students are less likely to learn.*

The fact is, you need to put effort into your room's appearance. I know this sounds obvious to many of you, but while it is a given amongst our elementary brethren, I find that as the students grow into their secondary classes, teachers devote less effort to the classroom environment. It's as if once the content gets more rigorous, the teacher can't seem to put the energy into what they believe to be the superficial coating. But I beg middle school teachers to keep the environment facade going strong. It feeds directly into a tween's sense of style, identity, and engagement. Sometimes we need to make changes without before changes can happen within. Isn't this the argument of every wardrobe makeover show or home cleanup reality TV program?

It's not that the learning environment is everything, but it accomplishes much more than many in education give it credit for accomplishing. The difference between the haves and have-nots in education is lessened in a school where the classrooms are equitable in their level of engagement. An engaging room helps to teach, surrounding students in evidence of the growing library of lessons of the year. An engaging room helps to build community (see Chapter 2 for more on this topic). Bottom line, an engaging room ultimately becomes a variable in the equation of student achievement.

So what does a tween-centric classroom look like? Well, this chapter explores these topics:

♦ The breakdown of a middle school classroom

♦ Keeping an aesthetically disorganized tween classroom

Look, for many of us, creating a tween-centric environment is somewhat of a designer's challenge. If you've ever seen a tween's bedroom at home, you'll know that to create a habitat that tweens want to reside in while still modeling organization and structure is an oxymoron.

But create it we must. It is our charge in both our teaching standards and what we know to be true: creating an engaging learning environment adds to student learning. In California, where I teach, in *Standards for Teaching* it states:

2.2 Creating physical or virtual learning environments that promote student learning, reflect diversity, and encourage constructive and productive interactions among students

- ♦ arrange and adapt classroom seating to accommodate individual and group learning needs
- ♦ establish a stimulating, curriculum-rich learning environment that supports content learning and academic vocabulary development
- ♦ ensure that students develop an appreciation of diversity
- ♦ provide students access to resources, technologies, and comfortable workspaces
- ♦ create an environment that promotes optimal learning for each student
- ♦ construct an equitable learning environment for all students

Consequently, we must organize our classroom and create a harbor of academic coolness that lures kids in with its siren's song and seduces them to learn.

The Breakdown of a Middle School Classroom

Many civilians are shocked to learn that that in August, when a teacher returns to his or her classroom, they are often greeted with a pile of furniture, poltergeist-style, stacked in the middle of the classroom from floor to ceiling. The carpets may have been vacuumed, true, but the classroom is far from ready to receive students. The walls are bare. In fact, many principals insist prior to summer vacation that the teacher strip the walls of all borders and backgrounds, not to mention student work or posters.

Every August I have to remind myself not to view this haphazard pile of chairs and desks and cabinets as a worker's comp application waiting to happen, but as an opportunity to redesign my classroom environment. I spend time reflecting on what it looked like in the past, and I ask myself the following two questions:

1. How is the layout and design going to help my instruction?

2. What can I live looking at for eight hours a day?

It's obvious why #1 is important, but don't dismiss #2. After all, it's not only about student achievement, but being a happier teacher, is it not? These students are coming into your "home," and if you don't think of it with pride, then they won't either.

Don't forget that although it's your home away from home, it is their home-away-from-home too, and in designing your classroom environment, you need to bring the tween into your thought process if you want to increase tween buy-in and care and maintenance of your room. It's always best to build a classroom out of the resilient materials of ownership and pride, which means bringing students into the discussion.

Therefore, allow your students input when you can. After all, sometimes they can design better for a tween audience than you can. For instance, at the end of each year I ask my Language Arts students for input in how the room should look when it greets my new students in the fall. I get ideas for boards, and even allow them to begin putting up basic boards so I can see what they are envisioning. Nine out of ten times, the students create catchier bulletin boards then I ever could, and that are set up to introduce a concept I taught ten months prior.

In other words, I'm sneaky. By asking students for advice on how the room should be in the following fall, I have also asked them to reflect and review concepts we covered ten months ago. Cue diabolical laughter.

To start your own brainstorming for creating a tween-centric classroom, I offer a blueprint of my own, complete with descriptions. It doesn't matter where you teach, what demographic, what time zone, age group, subject matter, or economic bracket, certain elements should be considered. I've taught third through twelfth grades in both inner-city and suburban schools. I've even home schooled a kid in a hotel on location for a movie. Each classroom I have taught in has had similar designated areas in their classroom habitat. Figure 1.1 shows my current middle school classroom in all its tween-crazed glory.

Figure 1.1. What My Classroom Looks Like

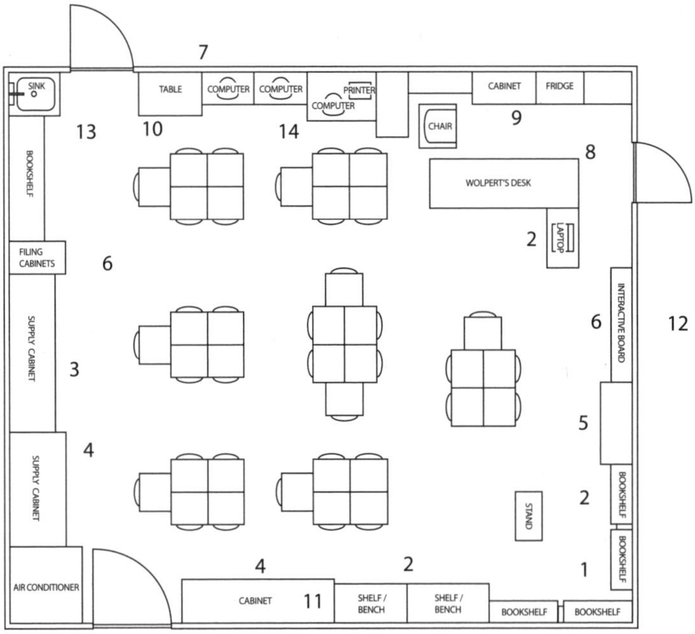

1. **Reading/Library Area**—Once you've read Chapter 8, it will come as no surprise that I believe a reading and library area, regardless of the subject you teach, should be the focal point of your classroom. Preferably, it should be in the front and unavoidable.

   Make your library area comfortable. Supply a couple of throw pillows from Target—and bada-bing-bada-bang—you've got yourself a place where kids want to hunker down and read. You'll also find that the pillows serve to lure kids closer to you from the back of the room.

2. **Sitting Area**—I know it's not Kindergarten and I'm not saying run out and go get carpet squares, but the space at the front of the room should be cleared to allow students closer access to you and your teachings. It sets a different tone in the room when kids are both at the desks and on pillows with clipboards in hands. I have also found that kids who are more squirmy or disruptive sitting at their desks, can sometimes function better when given choice of where to learn.

   For instance, I had two students who sat on the reading bench with clipboards, feet straight out in front of them, focused and participating. I had another student who did her best writing while standing at the podium. Others liked to hunker down in a corner or lie on their stomachs on a long pillow.

   It's about what's going to get the best out of them. They are more focused when allowed to differentiate their seat. Looking years down the line, even adults in the workplace believe that the cubicle-sitting-facing-the-same-sterile-wall-every-day environment is not conducive to their own achievement. When writing this very book, for instance, I paced, I sat outside with my laptop, I sat in my classroom, in my office, and at my dining room table. Why not allow students the same opportunity for choice by at least providing places in the room to choose from?

3. **Student Work Display**—I also want you to begin to think about the entire room as a student work display. It shouldn't just reside in one location, surrounded by a neat border. Involve students in the entire design of the room, and you will find that your efforts as a teacher will be reflected in their designs. My students have a say in the size of many of my displays and also do the actual execution. Students even create signatures at the bottoms of the displays to own the wall as their creation.

Make sure that regardless of who creates your student work wall that there is a step-by-step description up there of what it took to produce the assignment. Seamless learning may appear effortless or trite, but don't feel immodest in describing your students' efforts, or your own, right there on the display.

4. **Supplies/Storage Area**—There needs to be a place that is accessible by students. In fact, I have my students design the organization of our storage cabinets. Frankly, they do a better job than I do, and can recognize what needs the most attention. (See below for some organization ideas.)

5. **Content in Context Display**—In my room, there is always a small space on a designated wall that shows examples of how our content plays out in the real world. All it needs to be is on a small board or on a hanging chart or taped to the inside of a door.

There can be articles, photos, quotes, interviews, websites, etc., giving evidence of how your subject matter will apply later in life. Have students bring in examples as an assignment, and rotate who is in charge of the board each week. Have them hunt down *Where in the World...?* (Math appears, Language Arts is used, Science is reported) and students will be more likely to study the board when completed.

For instance, in Language Arts, it can be a book review when an author mentioned any of the narrative terms we talk about in class. In Science, it can be the announcement of a Nobel Prize winner. Regardless of the subject matter, bring the very room itself back to the all-important answer of "How does what we learn here apply to me later in life?" (See Chapter 5 for more on this topic.)

6. **Directed Instruction Areas**—I mentioned a sitting area in the front of the room, but also make sure that you have a place to teach in a directed instructional way at each wall or corner of the room. Especially if you teach in small groups or tables, it's important to rotate their perspective every so often. Have a chart on wheels or a mobile easel handy to move with you or to be where you intend to end your pacing.

By walking around or landing in a different part of the room to give your direct instruction from, the students will be more alert and more mentally absorbent. Besides, it allows you to see all of them from a new angle, and this alone helps in classroom management and engagement.

7. **Charts to Refer to Independently**—Keep charts handy. I love my Interactive whiteboard, really I do. However, I do miss having charts of brainstorms or lists created by the class to just rip off the easel and stick to the wall for future reference. There's something very concrete for a student in seeing a list created and posted. It reinforces the lesson to just see it there, having gone through the process of its creation. Keep the charts coming. Create and post, rip and stick, scribble and hang. Keep them up as long as you can before they become too much and anyone who walks into your room will see the learning process before them.

8. **My Center of the Globe**—This is my space, my place in the room that adds just a little distance between the students and myself when my airspace has been used up by the closeness of tweens. The tween room can get crowded, what with bodies, backpacks, books, and supplies, and they can be energy sapping. So claim a corner of the room and make it your own to take attendance or maybe just to crash into to answer one final question before the bell rings. Frankly, sometimes you just need a little physical distance to feel your batteries recharge.

   On the bulletin board above my desk are pictures of my family, drawings students have done of me or Shakespeare or me with Shakespeare, quotes, my college banner (Go Camels!), and important dates to remember—99% of the room is theirs; 1% is mine.

9. **Emergency Lesson Location**—Have a place where emergency lesson plans are accessible. Plan ahead. Have them printed out and stacked ready for use. (See Chapter 13 for advice on substitute teaching plans that aren't a total waste of time.)

10. **Folders for New Students**—Have some stapled packets already prepared for new students. You know the ones I mean, those students that appear in your classroom at each quarter end, or worse, the week before the state testing. Each document should have clear instructions when the piece is to be returned and include the following:

    ♦ My Introduction Letter including expectations, homework policy, grading policy, parent and student signature (Due: Next Day for full credit)

- Publishing (online and offline) permission slip for voice (podcasting), written work, and photographs (Due: Next Day for full credit)

- Movie/Clips permission slips for PG and PG-13 movies & or clips (Due: Next Day)

- School Schedule and Emergency Information (Due: Next Day)

- Reading Survey (Due: Two Days from first day in class)

- First Writing Piece (assignment varies) (Due: Three Days from first day in class)

11. **Weekly Agenda**—For $40, I had dry erase board mounted onto the doors of my cabinets. This gives me additional writing space. Remember that an interactive whiteboard takes up a huge chunk of wall. One cabinet is designated as the place where I write the weekly agenda, which I generally have planned before I leave the previous Friday. This allows me the weekend to have a life with my own family.

Every Monday, the class walks in and writes down the entire agenda. They color code in their agendas what I've color coded on the board: blue is class work and red means it's due on that day. The board isn't erased until Friday afternoon of that week.

The purpose of it all is to help the students with their time management. We're preparing them for high school and college, after all, and I believe in letting them see the overall scheme of things for the week so that they can plan accordingly. I get fewer excuses like, "I couldn't do my homework because it was my sister's birthday."

12. **Long Range Timeline**—This is an important element of the room. Remember when I said that you don't want to leave the students in the dark about what's to come? I take that a step further and have created an interactive bulletin board that is a timeline of each quarter.

Basically, the way it works is the students help by creating a timeline that was divided up into the weeks of the quarter. So one timeline might have ten divisions or so. I put icons that the students create on the approximate spot where a day off or vacation might be. I have icons for Reading assessments, Writing assessments, etc., so that the students can see where our assessments lie on our quarter timeline.

I have students go one step further and slap a sticky note on each of the days with details of that day's lessons so that kids who are absent or who just want to see when we learned something, can look at the growing lessons on the timeline. A tack represents the current day, and a student moves the tack as each day goes by. It's just another visual strategy to bring students into their own time management.

13. **Student Data Corner**—I've designated one of my doors as a place to hang student-created data. (See Chapter 4 for ideas on displaying in this area.) Basically, as class data changes, students create graphs and pie charts to track our improvement as a class.

14. **Tech Center**—I have three computers that I rescued from warehousing. Although they don't have the best, fastest, or most current systems around, and they are a bit Frankenstein in their rigging, our site technician is really supportive of trying to keep them on the district maintenance route. The kids have to hold the keyboards in their laps, but the computers work and are online for slow, but reliable, research or differentiation opportunities.

Although the foregoing is a description of the overall classroom environment, let's talk a little more specifically about how to organize things in the tween classroom so that you can keep track of papers, model organization, and keep your head above water. After all, you can drown in a tween classroom if you're not careful. Therefore, you have to develop a few ways to keep afloat of the mess, and in so doing, you will be modeling options for how your students can organize as well.

Keeping an Aesthetically Disorganized Tween Classroom

Let's face it, with the pace of Middle School, it's no wonder we aren't all buried in piles of papers, unused crates, dried out glue sticks, and student work. How to keep on top of the mess without staying at school every day until 9:00 PM takes learning tricks from some of those über-organized teachers who haunt every district. Not every teacher was born organized (case in point: yours truly), but if we expect quality in our student work, we have to model it ourselves, even if it isn't in our nature. We all have strengths, but sometimes knowing how to set up a tween-attractive room that is also organized is beyond even the best of teachers.

Being a tween, however, is a time of transition, and as we all know, transitions are times that signal great potential for disorganization. Therefore, despite the fact that it might not be our forte, we must model organization in order to be helping our tweens for their present and future challenges in school and beyond.

Being a tween, however, is a time of transition, and as we all know, transitions are times that signal great potential for disorganization.

Ray Bradbury said in his book, *Dandelion Wine*, that the grandma's kitchen was "organized chaos." I read that line for the first time when I was in eighth grade and it has stuck with me since. It seems to describe my state of being. It describes my own tween bedroom, my dorm room, and now, my classroom. To be organized in all the chaos takes some preparation on your part. You need to develop a way to keep the clutter down for easy filing or storing, and for easy access later.

My colleagues would be laughing at me right now to find that I'm actually giving advice on organization, but the fact is that although my room may look a little disheveled sometimes, the fact is that I know where things are and, more importantly, my students do too.

I will never be a superorganized teacher. I'm going to bet that if you're one of those die-cut, über-organized, not-one-paper-where-it-shouldn't-be kind of teacher, my level of tidiness (or lack thereof) will be offensive to you. I will say this, however: I am in awe of you and your fresh-smelling, plenty-of-room-to-walk-around-in classrooms. I wish that were in me, but it's not; and by admitting to myself that organization is not my best suit, I've taken the first step in developing strategies to help me still model organizational skills for my students, even if I myself do not excel at them by nature.

Here's what I have on hand to make keeping up with the middle school mess possible:

1. **Baskets**—This is the most aesthetic way to be disorganized. I use one in my library for books that kids are too lazy to return to the shelves. It's a compromise I make with some of them. If you aren't going to shelve them properly, then at least put them in the shelving basket. A student can earn community service hours for shelving them during lunch. At least it keeps the shelves attractive; and because my bigger goal is literacy, not popping a vein to make sure someone returned the book correctly, I pick my battles. Remember, the main thing is that the student borrowed the book in the first place, treated it carefully, and returned it to my library.

2. **Tupperware**—Easy, inexpensive way to organize supplies. You can buy the big stuff, the temporary stuff, the little bowls, and the big casserole dishes. Whatever is appropriate. You can tailor your storage solutions to your storage needs.

3. **File Folders**—I'm a little nutty about file folders. They're a little pricey, but you can staple them together to make desk carrels for test taking. You can hand one out to each student for portfolios without making them buy an entire binder. You can buy them in colors indicating any number of variables: classes, units, quarters, cooperative groups, etc. Buy a box and buy yourself a lot of space-saving heartache.

4. **Color Coding Stickers**—Color-coding is not just for elementary teachers. It's a way to indicate any number of categories, and with a key set up somewhere in a classroom, even the lowest level of students can follow your organizational instructions. I use them to indicate genres in my classroom library (see Chapter 8 for more on setting up your classroom library stacks). I use them to indicate which shelves are designated for which periods. I use them to help small groups find their supplies. I use them to help randomly group students. ("If the file you just pulled from the deck has a red sticker, go sit with your new group in the library for discussion. If yours is the color....") The possibilities are endless.

5. **Crates**—I love crates; just love 'em. They can be color coded to indicate different classes. They stack to save room. I mean, what can't you store in a crate? For instance, in my room, each Language Arts period has a crate. Inside the crate are files for each student in that period. Each file has a Test Prep, Works in Progress, and Portfolio folder. I always have an extra one handy to cart supplies outside if need be. I also use one that doubles for a mobile classroom library exchange if another teacher and I want to mix up our stacks a bit.

Bottom line, you have to be prepared for anything in a classroom as it comes up. So every August, you can find me, lurking through the aisles of office supply stores, a fiend for new organizational possibilities. I'll walk the aisles and look for other easy ways to label, sticker, or store, and buy a few new things that I can't even predict how they'll be used yet.

Remember, problems arise in tween classrooms by the hundreds that require quick problem solving. Sometimes, the solution is just a little supply cabinet check away.

Many's the time when I've heard the plea: "Mrs. W, where should I put these files after I've collected them?" To which I have replied, "Why don't you check in the cabinet up there and see if there's a crate waiting to be used?" Voila! Instructional time saved, and you become the organizational hero.

Every year I hope that I will become increasingly organized. But the process never ends. There are still piles, still things shoved under the proverbial carpet. However, it happens less and less as I try new strategies to stay on top of it all. Remember that teaching is a dusty and messy process as we roll around the content, getting our hands dirty with challenges. Things get lost and found, discarded one year and brushed off to try again another…just as it is with learning.

2

Tips for Building Community in the Middle School Classroom

Never doubt that a small group of thoughtful, committed citizens can change the world. Indeed, it is the only thing that ever has.
— Margaret Mead

Tweens thrive on tribes, cliques, clubs, organizations, and groups. Unfortunately, this is even the time of life where gangs may begin to rear their angry heads. We need to counterbalance the community a tween may have fallen into with the one created in our own classroom. The most powerful tool to keep the tween drama outside your door, and to keep the learning in, is to build community.

Spend time in the beginning of, as well as throughout, the year building the reputation that your class is *the* place to be. The effort to build community in your classroom will pay you back by making both your classroom management and your student achievement greater. In fact, by providing the clubhouse of learning for your students, you will also provide a common language for students who normally would not have hung out together. It becomes a shared experience that can span those tribes, cliques, clubs, organizations, groups, and gangs that exist outside your classroom.

Now, I'm not talking about taking time from instruction. I'm talking about putting in the groundwork to make instruction smoother and more effective. I'm not talking about straying from your content to do fluffy activities only seen at a campfire. I'm talking about injecting character into your content to build up some classroom pride. Remember, this book's about you, what's going to help your practice and make you happier. Building community in your classroom will make your students more comfortable, comfortable enough to make mistakes and learn from them, while making things easier on you, the tween teacher.

Therefore, we have to buy into their need for a clique, but just a little. Provide a place that is cool, but only if one is kind. Provide a place that is exciting, but only if one is inclusive. Provide a place that is fun, but only if one is appropriate. Provide a place that allows students to be the best of themselves, and you'll never have to see the worst of each kid.

This chapter discusses these topics:

- Why go through the trouble of building community?

- Building small groups

- Building consensus

- Sentence stems for praising and critiquing our peers

- More community-building activities

We've all been in classrooms where kids don't clap for each other, literally. And we've all been in classrooms where they celebrate each other's smallest accomplishments. You want the latter because it will be a place where they give their best for you, for their peers, and for themselves.

Why Go Through the Trouble of Building Community?

Building community is vital for achievement and social development, one of the most important and effective teaching tools that you can use for tween learning. It creates a stability that many tweens crave during this time in their lives, and it creates a comforting echo that they may seek out again, even beyond your walls.

Kati Delahanty, a member of the Edutopia.org National Advisory Board and high school English teacher in the Boston public school system is an authority on building community in teenage classrooms. When I asked her why it's important to build community in the tween and teen classroom, she replied as follows:

Building community is particularly important for tweens and teens because of how insecure and vulnerable many young people feel throughout their adolescence. Building community is about building a safe space wherein real learning can happen. When students feel comfortable with their peers, they are more willing to take risks, to make mistakes, and to allow themselves to embrace the learning process—which, as we know, is messy and imperfect.

Just take note: Make sure that you don't build community at the expense of other classrooms. You are looking for students to love being in your classroom, but not necessarily to *not* love being in other classrooms. Don't downplay another teacher's classroom environment in an attempt to build up your own classroom community. Rather, allow the tribe that begins in your classroom to ripple out to involve the school community, thus spreading the wealth. Build a community that is neighborly, not one that is exclusive. Otherwise, you've created just another middle school clique.

Some teachers make their classroom the place for students to hang out in during their free time. They open up their classroom for lunch, after school, etc. Personally, I find I like a little tween-free lunch for some adult time to recharge my batteries so that I'm better when class begins again. However, opening up your classroom during their free time is a great way to encourage comfort in your classroom, and there's nothing like the feeling that kids are spreading the word about your room. This is indicated by the fact that kids begin trailing in with their friends who are not your actual students. You meet more kids from other classrooms that way, and that builds school community.

Building community isn't just about everyone feeling all yummy at school, it is really meant to build achievement. If it didn't, I may as well be a counselor at a day camp. The fact is that I'm not talking about building such a comfortable environment it isn't rigorous. This isn't about making it so engaging that you've trained students to only work hard at what they find entertaining. I'm talking about creating an environment that encourages the comfort to challenge oneself and fail, the comfort to ask others for advice and criticism, and the comfort to reflect on what worked and what didn't in a way that supports improvement.

Don't let the naysayers fool you. The fact is that to build community in the classroom takes guts for a teacher. After all, when tweens interact anything can happen. So it takes a brave and consistent educator with clear goals for themselves and clear scaffolding for their students to begin the process.

I begin creating community right in my classroom on day one. Then I continue by building community-supporting activities into my curriculum throughout the school year. As a result, if you were to look through a window into my classroom, you would see evidence of a deep community that ultimately helps with everything from smiles to scores.

A place of strong community means a place where students share their mistakes with humor, not horror.

You'd see students working in small groups without me hovering around them. You'd see different students from different outside cliques working side by side, advising each other and learning from each other. You'd see the brooding quiet kid standing up to offer his latest piece of writing. You'd hear students praising the good in that piece with honesty before giving equally honest advice in a way that the advice-receiving student can hear. Lastly, you'd hear laughter—comfortable laughter, not someone-being-made-fun-of laughter—and for tweens, it's important that they know the difference.

A place of strong community means a place where students share their mistakes with humor, not horror. It means tweens who can be paired comfortably with each other, no matter whom they are assigned. It means students who seek answers from each other before seeking them from me. It means classmates who celebrate the victories of the class and their accomplishments in addition to their own individual successes.

It's harder, but there are rewards to putting in the constant effort, and there are lessons and activities that can help you cut down on the building time and quickly vitalize the classroom community.

Building Small Groups

The basic building block of a classroom community needs to be the small groups that you construct throughout your year. Many teachers now use small groups, maybe for a particular purpose like a specific project or workshop program, but there are still teachers who continue to use rows and the more straightforward classroom structure as a means create authority in the room. I challenge you, however, to use small groups as your norm. It is your first step to creating the tight-knit group of students that will make up your classroom community.

The fact is, you want those middle schoolers to leave their drama outside your door in exchange for the neighborhood you created within your doors. If you want those kids to be able to work together, help each other, and be comfortable around each other, you've got to shake up your classroom structure. Students can't spend their day only looking and interacting with you upfront and still be expected to know how to interact with each other.

Here are some routines and activities you can do to support the foundation of your classroom community:

1. **Create Table Jobs**—There are ways to manage small group activities that involve assigning roles to the members of the group. Regardless of the topic or subject being discussed, the roles can be rotated for each new day or week, etc. Figure 2.1 shows how to break down jobs for a small table group.

   With each activity, interacting in small groups will get increasingly easier. And remember that if our goal is to prepare the students for their futures, we have to remember that their future outside of school will be far more collaborative than ours will be. Help them by giving them the practice to interact as a community.

Figure 2.1. Table Jobs

Messenger—this is the only person who can raise his/her hand (after the group has agreed on the question or solution) or get supplies for the group	
Artist–Illustrator/Grapher, etc.—creates the visual associated with the activity	Presenter—this person does the actual final presentation in front of the class
Manager—watches the group's times and deadlines, breaks ties	Reporter—record on a template each person's contributions to a discussion as a means to report to me about the goings on in the group

2. **Have Those Small Groups Move**—This can be scary for some, but you have to disrupt your seating chart repeatedly. While my students sit in the small groups daily, every week or so they rotate their positions. That's because some positions have greater influence on the group than other positions. The head of the table needs to switch. Also, this means that kids interact with a wider variety of classmates. Their perspective of the classroom changes, their view changes, and how they relate to each other also subtly changes.

3. **Name the Small Table Groups**—The first thing we do when we begin a new unit is to name our table groups. This builds an even smaller community within our greater classroom community. The names must be reached by consensus, and must relate to the curriculum. To identify the group, students have to design a table tent that uses both linguistic and nonlinguistic representations, teacherese for "it has to have words and pictures" (Figure 2.2, page 18).

4. **Fluid Grouping**—Each desk within each table group has an assigned name in accordance with our curriculum. For instance, I label each of the desks in a table with a character in literature. It's just my way of further integrating my content. Whatever your content, name your desks: for example, Pythagoras, Mycenae, ∏, or Perimeter; go to town. Figure 2.3, page 18, diagrams one such table group.

Figure 2.2 Table Names

Figure 2.3. A Table Group

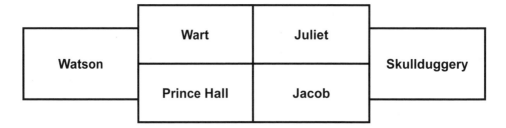

Watson	Wart	Juliet	Skullduggery
	Prince Hall	Jacob	

By labeling the desks at the table groups, I can create easy fluid groups. Fluid groups are ever changing small groups that are set up to lose no instructional time when morphing. I can say things like:

"All Juliets please go get your table's Works in Progress folders."

"All Warts get together to decide on a thesis statement."

"During this silent read, could I see all Skullduggeries over here for a brief meeting?"

It's all about integration opportunities and making the most out of every moment of instructional time. It's also about mixing up the students with fluidity, and creating a tighter community. And that community will help your class run more efficiently.

So you've built the groups, flipped them, moved them, named them, and surprised them, but now you need to teach the students how to talk and discuss within those groups. This is the next step in building a community for the classroom as a whole.

Building Consensus

Once you buy-in to small groups, you have to teach them the language of getting along. As we know, problem solving requires making decisions, and making decisions in a community (even a small group of five) and reaching consensus with a group is hard even for adults. Now imagine you're a middle schooler in a group that consists of someone you have a crush on, someone you hate, someone who's shy, and someone who's overbearing. Your teacher gives you a task and a timed deadline and says, "Solve!"

It wouldn't be fair and it wouldn't be effective. Consequently, scaffolding how to be fair in a group or small groups won't work. I really feel for teachers who excuse their failure to use this powerful strategy by claiming that small group work isn't fair to the high achievers or that it somehow allows under-achievers to continue to float under the radar. These aren't sufficient reasons to not tackle that which makes a richer environment. Rather, they are reasons to solve those problems instead.

To reach a consensus requires work from every member of the group and a way to hold each group member accountable. Let's consider an example from my own classroom.

My guided question was "Do you believe in paying students for their good grades? Why or why not?" The small groups had to come to an agreement, make a decision, and produce an essay, written by the entire group, to convince me of their opinion.

1. Have the students each write a paragraph stating their opinion and their most important reason.

2. Pass around these papers amongst the members of the group so that each member reads everyone's contributions and everyone has input.

3. Have someone tally students' opinions to determine what the majority believes.

4. Allow someone from the minority opinion to make a final argument.

5. Vote one at a time: ballots, show of hands, etc.

6. Move on as soon as the decision has been made.

In this way, each student becomes responsible for writing one of the paragraphs in the persuasive essay. Then have the groups mount their paragraphs onto a small poster and share the posters with the rest of the class. See? Individual accountability and small group work. It can be done!

Other ways to make decisions may not involve agreement, but they can still involve the group. A team leader can hear both sides and make a decision. If you're in a real bind and really need the tween arguments to just stop already, a representative from each side can do Rock-Paper-Scissors. Elementary you say? Sure. But remember, the benefit of teaching students who have one foot in elementary school and one foot in high school is that you can use strategies from both worlds. And if you don't want to use a three-out-of-four method, an impartial party from another group can be brought in. A tween Switzerland, if you will.

Teaching kids how to communicate builds communication. Hence, the shared root word.

Sentence Stems for Praising and Critiquing Their Peers

Go farther than you might expect with scaffolding their discussions. After all, we can't expect students to just know how to talk maturely to each other unless we teach it. Otherwise conversations will descend into tween drama or unproductive disagreements.

Teach how to appropriately disagree. Model how to praise honestly, not just to make their best friend feel good. Give your students the language to talk to each other in a true and productive community.

One way to scaffold giving feedback is to use a method called "Three Stars and a Wish" (Figure 2.4). This can, of course, be altered to suit your needs, but basically, the instruction asks that on an index card, the student must give three compliments before making a wish for the peer's next steps. This can be used when students critique each other's essays, word problems, lab findings, etc.

Figure 2.4. Three Stars and a Wish

★ Great vocab! Good choice of words.

★ Fantastic job giving back ground information in
introduction paragraph

★ Hitting key points in the story to help back up
your topics

~~~~~~~~~~~~~~~

I wish that you use better transitions rather than
bringing up a topic out of the blue.

But to fill the index card, students need even further guidance at first. After all, one isn't born being able to critique diplomatically. Just check out this typical critique from one tween to another sans guidance:

Dude, this sucks.

However, with proper teaching and scaffolded sentence stems and fragments provided, a student can instead say:

Perhaps you could add a thesis statement to improve this writing?

Model using the following stems and fragments. You can even provide a reference sheet with them on it for students to refer to, if necessary, to help them give appropriate written or verbal feedback and advice.

Here are some common sentence stems and language possibilities to help guide their discussions so you are in the presence of a group of students who actually sound like a community of learners.

- ◆ To disagree:
  - "I realize not everyone will agree with me, but…"
  - "That's an interesting idea, but maybe…"
  - "I see it a little differently because…"
- ◆ To agree:
  - "I agree with what _____ said about…"
  - "I was wondering/thinking about that too."

- To encourage community from a fellow student
  - "_____we haven't heard from you yet."
  - "Could you give me an example of that?"
  - "Could you repeat/rephrase that?"
- To make sure you're all on the same page
  - "In other words, you think that…[paraphrase], right?"
  - "Can I just take that point a step further and say that…?"
- To help solve/add to the thought
  - "May I add something here?"
  - "Maybe you could…"
  - "Perhaps you could…"

Give them the tools to talk with respect and they will help you create a room that functions with respect.

More Community-Building Activities in a Tween Classroom

Think about your own family and how it takes effort to make it work during the best and worst of times. With every get-together, every holiday, every weekend, it takes effort and building community to feel like a successful unit. It's ongoing. So it is with building community in a classroom. Here are some more activities to use throughout your school year to continue the achievement and the more efficient functioning of your class:

1. **Make Time for Group Problem-Solving Activities**—Have students work in groups to put jigsaw puzzles together. Give them a set time to do it, then have them reflect on the different methods and strategies they used to accomplish their goal. Give them political cartoons to analyze together, or mysteries to solve. It builds up both community and critical-thinking skills all in one short and engaging activity that you should make time for again and again.

2. **Create "Academic Allies"**—As Delahanty does, "pair students up so that they have one person to check-in with each day, to collaborate with, and to learn to support academically." I have them write their phone numbers and/or email address in their agendas so that they can call on each other outside of school. I also mix up these pairings on a regular basis.

3. **Table Representatives**—In a discussion, it's always great to elect a representative to share out the results after batting around possibilities. This not only sets a limit on the number of voices in a debate, but you'll find kids sitting on their desktops to get a glimpse of their representative like moms in a toddler beauty pageant.

For instance, I asked a question of my students during our Persuasive Writing Unit, "Are same-sex schools valuable in education?" I gave each group time to discuss, come to a consensus, and choose a representative. In a strategy I learned at the Writing Project, I handed out a sign to each representative that read, "Agree" on one side and "Disagree" on reverse. With great flair, and on the count of three, I had the reps display the sign that reflected their group's decisions. Then one by one, those students were permitted to give their best argument.

As for the kids sitting back in the table groups, you'll find that they cheer each other on, applauding at their rep's responses. As long as you can stand the learning buzz going on in the classroom and don't demand absolute silence, this activity may be the one for you.

Again, this activity works just as well in describing the solution to a math problem or using the scientific method to come to a hypothesis; of course, any historical debate also can use this method of community discussion.

4. **Author's Chair**—Tweens love to show off. Author's chair is one way to give them that opportunity. This is an activity in any classroom that can be used to showcase when students want to share their writing, their results, their conclusions, and their thought processes.

Designate a place in each room that a student goes to share his or her thoughts with the class. At the end of an activity, have students volunteer to go to that location and share their writings or findings with the class. After each share, model how to praise and how to challenge that student. This also allows for your own differentiated assessment of each student. Have students clap for everyone. Students, after all, need to find ways to communicate honest praise regardless of the level of writing or the level of sharing. Even the lowest-achieving student who shares out should be praised for being a part of that which was a struggle for him or her.

Now, the key with the author's chair is to offer it often. I can't stress this enough: the more often you find time to do this, the better. Use it as an exit card in the last five minutes of class or as an icebreaker in the first five minutes. The fact is, the Author's Chair isn't just an assessment of the work they're doing; their willingness to participate is an assessment of the level of community that currently exists in your classroom. If they are comfortable with each other, they will share. If there are no willing takers, keep working on it.

5. **Let the Students Design the Classroom**—(See Chapter 1 for some more detailed information on this subject.) Have the students own their classroom by making them stakeholders in its appearance. Have them put up the bulletin boards or at least be instrumental in their design. Ask them their opinion of what's working, what's grabbing their eye, what tool they are using, and what has become a blur. I even have students create advertisements for the academic content to hang in my classroom. For instance, taking a tip from those dramatic iPod ads (you know the ones of the black silhouettes on the bright-colored backgrounds), I have the kids design posters that reflect the curriculum we're studying (see Chapter 8 for a more detailed description of this project). When done at the beginning of the year, the activity breaks the ice and the students own a little more of my classroom having designed our décor. It's not unlike stapling a poster on a clubhouse wall, except in this case it's my classroom.

6. **Classroom Competitions**—Some would say that competitions are not in the community spirit. I would respond that they are, if you're teamed by classroom. That is, if you can design a willing academic competition between classes, it works to build community within those classrooms. Now, I'm not talking about *Survivor* or anything similar; I'm talk about competition that builds content as well as community.

For instance, my classes' essay-writing nemeses are the classes of Room 4. Kenna McRae, a brilliant colleague of mine, has a background in special education and a closet of props and costumes for any reading genre. She designed persuasive writing competitions between our mainstream classes some time ago when we took on the Great Debate: Batman vs. Superman. My students set out to prove that Batman was the more interesting character, while McRae's class stood firm in their resolve that Superman was the most interesting of the two.

For a couple of years, the writing, exchanging of papers, and teacher proclamations were enough, but recently, we outsourced the scoring of our competing essays. As a by-product, the feeling of involvement, or community, of being a part of something special rippled out as well. Instead of scoring each other's essays, we recently involved a third classroom, that of our wonderful colleague Suzie Menerey, whose students scored our Batman vs. Superman persuasive essays using the district rubric. This third class also created certificates of award and participation for each student who wrote an essay. They designed a proclamation for the winning class (McRae's, incidentally) and gave feedback. All the classes involved talked about the competition in the classroom and outside the classroom. Thus, the community rippled out further, beyond the walls of my room, building a broader neighborhood.

7. **Use Circles for Large Group Discussion**—Kati Delahanty is a huge supporter of shoving the furniture aside and forming a big circle for large-group discussion. Her reasoning was lost on me until she said the following:

   "The importance and power of circles comes from the fact that it is an equal way to participate….Each person has the opportunity to be heard and to speak *without* interruption. Sitting in an actual circle (with no tables in the way) opens each person up to being vulnerable. It's important mostly because it is a practice in listening, in being present, and in supporting the members of your community."

   What is also true is that mixing it up, pushing aside the normal sitting arrangement, and making students work together, talk together, and plan together on a consistent, ongoing basis will add to their sense of group self. It will aid their practice in that they will develop group ownership of their learning, which, in turn, will improve achievement.

8. **Digital Storytelling**—Kids aren't born appreciating other people's sagas. And when they hit those tween years, they can be unforgiving if we haven't specifically targeted empathy as a life skill. Additionally, there's a by-product of teaching about other people's backgrounds: it builds community.

   Digital Storytelling helps in assessing their twenty-first century skills and in teaching narrative. Give students a camera, some editing software, and some license-free music and watch them tell the stories of their life, the stories in their heads, and the stories of each other. Pair them off and conduct interviews and then screen the films for the entire class. Create a Sundance Film Festival in your very own classroom, sans the paparazzi.

9. **Teach them to Juggle**—I'm not kidding. Well, I'm kind of kidding. Teach students a little known skill, and you'll find that they gather in groups during their off time to practice it together. One physical education teacher at my school brought in some hacky sacks and taught our middle schoolers a few kicks. The result was that playing with hacky sacks took off! We found little hacky sack learning communities all over campus that would just grow, and more and more students joined in. It created an active community. Juggling, those Chinese yo-yo things, whatever. Give them a strange skill to focus on in their down time.

10. **Courtesy Contract**—Remember when I said that building community is an ongoing process? Well, even toward the end of the year I am working to fine tune and tweak their respect of each other, the classroom, of education, and, ultimately, of themselves.

And that's the key. If you can find ways for students to be leaders, to surprise themselves in their own abilities, and to respect themselves, then your impact as a teacher will extend beyond your classroom and the year you had with them.

The Courtesy Contract is a very special activity I save for the end of the year. Let me back up. In my classroom library sit two tomes, huge books of contracts that students, more than 2,200 students ranging in age from eleven to eighteen years old, have contributed to. These pages represent contracts, promises that my students have made to try to be decent in their lives beyond my classroom. They vow to take the feeling they've had here, and remember what it felt like when they are tested later in life. I save the contract for the end of the year for two reasons:

1. They must feel community deeply in the classroom already to create the contract with the depth that I need them to.

2. I want to set them up for success. If they made promises at the beginning of the year and then broke them simply as a consequence of being a tween, then the contract will hold less meaning for them. By leaving it until the end, students know they have left something of themselves with me that hasn't

been corrupted by the normal mistakes of growing up. It resonates with them more.

Of course, I model my own courtesy contract before asking them to write one. By modeling my own, and by showing them the buy-in from all of the other students over the years, they always write the best damn pledge of their tween lives.

Does every student end up changing his or her life in my classroom? Of course not. But you want to build Camelot, a place where, "for one brief shining moment," they thought they could be the best they could be wherever they went. And if they fall short of that goal? Who cares. Falling short at least meant that they reached higher than they had before they tried. I leave you with some excerpts from some random Courtesy Contracts that have been turned in through the years, beginning with an example of my own (Figure 2.5) and followed by excerpts from student contracts (Figure 2.6, page 28).

Figure 2.5. My Courtesy Contract

I, Heather Wolpert-Gawron, do hereby vow to be the best teacher, wife, and mother I can be. I pledge to continue my own education so that I can always teach my students in ways that help them, challenge them, and prepare them for their futures. I promise to try to be a wife who chooses her battles so that my husband and I don't fight over silly things like who gets to choose the next Wii game. I promise to be my son's first teacher. I pledge to challenge myself in life, for "a life lived in fear is a life half-lived." But I also promise to never jump out of a plane again. I know I did it to challenge myself, but what was I thinking?! I can't promise that every classroom lesson will be yippie-yahoo-fun, but I do vow to sharpen my teaching practice like a knight with a sword, year after year; and when the time comes that I don't enjoy teaching, I will gracefully leave the classroom, waving my hand like a Homecoming Queen. I promise to push through the difficulties of life, reminding myself that everything's temporary. But I also vow to try to linger in the good chapters of life, cherishing them so that I can remember them when times get tough. I pledge this on this day, _____.

Signed. _____

Figure 2.6. A Sampling of Student Excerpts from Courtesy Contracts

I SWEAR to not be abusive to my one day future family. I will try to contribute to the world as much as possible, and keep a straight face when someone falls, even if I am cracking-up inside. Life will give me challenges and I will have to accept the duel. I

I pledge to remain that way. But most of all, I pledge to always stay truthful and loyal to my family and maybe set a better example for my younger brother and sister so I could show them things that my parents could not. I pledge this today, on June 13th, 2006.

When someone is in need, I will try my best to help them. ~~When someone is in need, I~~ I promise to keep my grades at an honor level. When it comes to fights, I will learn to resolve it with words, not violence. I vow not swear as much. I also promise to never take or try drugs. I pledge to finish high school and go to college. I'll try to respect my elders and learn from them. I promise to become someone people look up to, for all the great things I will do. Instead of being on television or news for killing, robbing, or doing something stupid, I'll be on for suceeding of doing a good deed. I pledge to see

in a gang. I'll try not to lie or curse. I promise not to get into a fight. If and when I do ever get into a fight I promise to be the bigger person and use words instead of fists. I will not give into peer pressure and not argue with my family. I will try to do my best at everything. I vow to respect everyone even those who don't deserve it. I promise to maintain good grade.

3

Tips for Teaching Tweens About Their Brains and How They Learn

See, the human mind is kind of like...a piñata. When it breaks open, there's a lot of surprises inside.

— Jane Wagner

Please circle the correct response.

What are tweens most interested in?

A. World History between the years of 400 BC and 1400 AD

B. How to write a literary analysis essay on the theme of "Number the Stars"

C. The definition of the term *quadratic equation*

D. Themselves

Answer: D

Figure 3.1. The Average Tween Brain

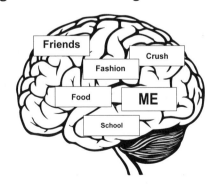

It should come as no surprise that the most intriguing topic to a middle schooler is middle schoolers (Figure 3.1). I can't blame them. Their bodies are changing. Their priorities are changing. Their identities are mutating as fast as their bone structure, and they want to know about where they are going to land after their morphing is done, both mentally and physically. More importantly, they want to know how what we teach relates to them, not as people, but as tweens.

Look at it this way: Your teaching every year is like a narrative, and there comes to be a B-story that tween teachers need to own in their lesson design. If the A-story is the standards-based content, then the B-story is the tween-based content, and there is a huge difference between a middle school classroom run by a teacher who takes on this added curriculum and a middle school classroom whose teacher doesn't. It's the difference between silver and gray.

I must confess that there was a time when I was jealous of the health teacher. I mean those kids *loved* going to that class, couldn't wait to get there, and kept talking about the content all day long. It wasn't just because she was teaching them about sex and drugs. OK, I'm delusional. Maybe that was some of it. But the bottom line was that she talked to them about them, and the minute I realized that there was a way to tap into this excitement by just shoving my standards-based curriculum over to share the target with tween-centric lessons, my students soon felt that same way about my Language Arts class.

So I began to become something more than a teacher, I realized that I also needed to become a hobbyist in what a tween was and what made a tween tick. Furthermore, I had to make sure that I didn't keep my findings to myself, but allowed them access to the knowledge as well.

I began by infusing my own professional development with brain research. Specifically, how the tween brain works. I mean, if my job is to teach to it, I felt I should know more about it. In so doing, my practice evolved and continues to evolve.

> **My class became focused on not just what to learn, but how best to learn it.**

My class became focused on not just what to learn, but how best to learn it. It became a class that taught students that they could, by using certain strategies, leave my classroom with greater intelligence than when they entered it, because they could control their own depth of learning.

It's this concept of "control" that's so fascinating to middle schoolers, for in every other aspect of their lives they are out of control. They wake up with different faces than the ones they went to sleep with, marked by zits while they slept. They don't drive but they want to go places. They can't get a worker's permit, but they need cash. Meanwhile, many adults tell them that they are too old for this but not old enough for that. Consequently, to realize that there is something that they can control—their own level of learning—is empowering. It's empowering for them to feel their level of intellect is in their hands and isn't a hand they were just dealt at birth. It's also empowering for the teachers to know that any student they get in the fall can have the ability to grow by the spring. All it takes is teaching tweens about what makes them tick and how they can tick better.

So this chapter discusses these topics:

♦ Understanding how the tween brain learns

♦ Tips for the tween brain to learn better

♦ Teaching brain-centric activities

♦ Further research

I need to be frank, however. I'm not going to be able to teach you deeply about the tween brain here. I'm not a neurologist. What I am going to do is make an argument, hopefully a darn good one, as to why you should educate yourself further about it. And I'll give you some resources to learn from.

The best resource I've found for brain research in regard to education is by Judy Willis. Willis, a neurologist turned teacher, makes understanding all this stuff really relatable to the classroom. If ever you have the chance to hear her speak, get thee to a Willis workshop, pronto. You'll learn tons. Her books include:

♦ *How Your Child Learns Best: Brain-Friendly Strategies You Can Use to Ignite Your Child's Learning and Increase School Success* (Naperville, IL: Sourcebooks, 2008)

♦ *Research-Based Strategies to Ignite Student Learning: Insights from a Neurologist and Classroom Teacher* (Alexandria, VA: ASCD Publishing, 2006)

♦ *Inspiring Middle School Minds: Gifted, Creative, & Challenging* (Scottsdale, AZ: Great Potential Pr., Inc., 2009)

One of the most important points she makes is that people are not born at a certain intelligence level and stay that way. It's a common and horrible misconception people have that somehow our intelligence levels can't be changed. Hogwash. Intelligence is not gifted at birth, unalterable; and when students realize that they can alter their brain, it is absolutely empowering, like realizing for the first time that you aren't shackled for life to remain in the house you were born in. That with work and development, you can dream of other futures and one day move out.

> *Intelligence is not gifted at birth, unalterable; and when students realize that they can alter their brain, it is absolutely empowering.*

This very myth feeds into the insecure world of a middle schooler. To take from them that false burden of "that's just the way it is," is liberating. Anything you can do to help tweens feel more secure in their abilities and possibilities will potentially improve their achievement in your classroom.

Anything you can do to make tweens feel more in control becomes a powerful tool for you and for them.

For this machine that is their brain is a tool, and it is one that, although it came to them from the factory all nice and new, can still be modified and souped up. Teach them to pimp their brain.

The tween brain is different developmentally from that of elementary students and of high schoolers, and it must be treated as such. Even though we teach to the standards, our lessons should still reflect the existing solid science that proves how the brain learns best at this stage of development. For if we want what we teach to be embedded into long-term memory instead of being discarded from short-term memory, we need to create lessons that send it to the area of the brain reserved for long term use.

Understanding How the Tween Brain Learns

First, are some words to know that will make you sound really smart with your students. Here's a secret: If it seems that you know more about tweens than the tweens do, they'll pay even greater attention to what you have to say. Imagine that this is the Cliff Notes of tween brain research. However, your research should not stop here because, frankly, the more you know about how tweens learn, the more you can pass on to them the secrets of how they process and embed knowledge. In the end, this leads to greater achievement.

Some key words to know:

♦ **Prefrontal Cortex**—This part of the brain makes up only 17% of the brain and is in charge of judging, analyzing, categorizing, organizing, deciding on fact or opinion, connecting the dots between how concepts relate to each other, and making calls on what is valid information and what isn't. It also plays a huge role in empathy and self-awareness. Yet this is one of the last parts of the brain to develop, and as such, still in flux and able to be influenced. But because the tween brain is not yet fully developed, hormones and emotions easily manipulate the prefrontal cortex.

Let me repeat that: hormones and emotions. Sound familiar? Yep. The middle school brain.

So in other words, just when we're asking them to judge and show relationships, evaluate, and analyze, the middle schooler's prefrontal cortex can be sidetracked in a big way simply by a note slipped to them during the passing period. It's not that they can't control it, but to know this gives a student power to work despite it. They can overcome their tendencies if they know what their tendencies are, just as we can better fight an enemy if we know the enemy we are facing.

♦ **Automatic Brain**—This is also known as the reactive brain and makes up the remaining 83% of the brain. Just as the word "automatic" implies, it's the part of the brain that automatically reacts to the world around it. In other words, when a student is stressed, depressed, angry, or just plain bored, information gets filtered into the reactive brain, not the prefrontal cortex, possibly dooming that information to the short-term memory, temporary storage.

Consequently, when we think about middle schoolers, we know that for many of them: stress, depression, anger, and boredom can be completely out of whack and disproportionate, so it becomes essential that we design lessons that help coax information into the prefrontal cortex.

♦ **Neurons**—A neuron is a nerve cell that transmits information along the nervous system. Neurons are connected by synapses. Think of it like neurons are the train depots and the synapses are the trains upon which the information is carried.

♦ **Neuroplasticity**—If you have students break down this word, they'll figure it out for you before you even have to define it for them. This term refers to the very encouraging fact that the brain is capable of growth, of developing new connections and pathways between neurons through new experiences and teachings. In other words, if a bridge is down between the train depots (see above), specially targeted lessons might just help build track where there was none before.

♦ **Dopamine**—This is a neurotransmitter, a chemical that is released as a feel-good drug for the brain. When a person feels pleasure, success, or pride, dopamine is released into the brain and acts as a lubricant of sorts, increasing attention, motivation, and memory. (Incidentally, when you first mention the word "dopamine" as the feel-good drug, you might keep your eye on the kids who titter at the "dope" part, shooting looks across the room at their buddies. It might give you some information about them and their outside hobbies. It's not evidence of use, by any means, but your antennae should always be up, gathering information about how they learn or what may be hindering their learning.)

- **Amygdala**—This is the part of the brain that monitors the emotions. Although we think of feelings being located in the heart, it's actually the amygdala that decides, based on the emotion a person feels, where to send information. If the person is stressed, freaked, scared, and freezes up, information gets routed by the amygdala to the reactive brain, avoiding the path to the sacred long-term memory storage.

- **Hippocampus**—This is the area of the brain next to the amygdala that creates connections between prior learning and experiences with information. Creating relationships between new information and past information preps the new piece for long-term memory storage.

- **Reticular Activating System (RAS)**—This is the first stop in a piece of information's possible categorization in the brain. Unconsciously, the RAS system sorts though billions of bits of information per second and organizes them by something that should be considered at a later time and something that can be immediately discarded. As a teacher, you want to make sure your lessons get through the RAS filter, and pass its test of what's worth keeping.

- **"Syn-naps"**—Judy Willis coined this great term for taking little brain breaks and allowing the brain to replenish and take a breather of sorts. Through her studies, she has discovered that every ten minutes a teacher should switch activities or modalities, create suspense, or do something spontaneous in order for brains to shake the doldrums away.

But this vocabulary doesn't tell you everything you need to know. It tells you the team players, but not the structure of the game. So to understand how it all works (in a very, ultrasimple, über elementary way) let's do a little visualization here. Let's say there's this bit of information that a student needs to know for their unit test in eighth grade History. Here it is:

In 1858, Abraham Lincoln delivered his famous "House Divided" speech.

The student, let's say her name is Alex, sits in class with her elbow on the desk and her cheek in her hand as the words are uttered by the teacher. The words go floating through the air and into Alex's ear. The fact passes through the eardrum (#1 in Figure 3.2) and into the brain through one of those metal camera-lens-like-closing-doors from *Star Wars*. Whoosh! Door closes behind it.

The fact, "In 1858, Abraham Lincoln delivered his famous 'House Divided' Speech," then travels into the RAS filtering system. RAS isn't paying much attention. She's reading a newspaper, sipping coffee, and offhandedly just sorts information into two piles: "to be trashed" and "still to be considered."

Luckily our little fact has joined the latter pile, but the system is totally on overload right now and the fact is asked to take a number and have a seat in the waiting room outside. After all, the student has other things to think about. She didn't have breakfast, her best friend passed her a note during the passing period saying, "whatever he says, don't believe it," and her boyfriend slipped her a note during class saying, "I didn't kiss her, I promise." She also hasn't started her 3D cell project that is due Friday, and she wonders if her mom will be able to take her to the store to get some Styrofoam or if she has to make it out of her younger sister's Play-Doh again this year.

Figure 3.2. Journey of a Piece of Information

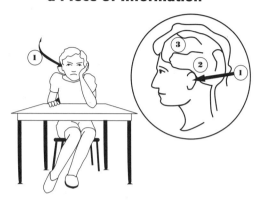

"The amygdala will see you now," a neuron says, and finally ushers the fact through the next Swoosh! door (#2 in Figure 3.2) to the next filter that determines if it's a worthy enough piece of information to get through the velvet rope to the prefrontal cortex.

Suddenly, the student takes a deep breath, shakes her head, and realizes that she's been phasing out in class. She reaches into her backpack and secretly sneaks some granola from her lunch, allowing the crunch and the food to wake her up a little. She takes a swig of water and hydrates her mouth and system, sits up straight, and the fact is then given the go ahead, and ushered into the next phase of processing.

Meanwhile, as soon as the fact has greeted the amygdala, the hippocampus gets to work trying to find connections between this new piece of information and any prior knowledge that Alex might have stored in her long-term memory. "Ah! Here's a file about Abraham Lincoln that she's had since fifth grade when she did that project on President's Day!" the hippocampus says. A connection made, the new fact begins to feel more confident that the prefrontal cortex is in sight and picks up speed.

What strategies can we teach students to help them purposely shake off the daydreams and proactively attack a case of having a tween moment?

The student raises her hand and says, "In fifth grade I learned that a doctor named Mudd helped Lincoln's assassin with his leg during his getaway. And now we have the phrase 'your name will be mud' because people were so mad that he helped the guy." The students laugh a bit, some say they remember that too, and the teacher says thanks for that little factoid tid-bit. Alex feels good, and some dopamine is released into the brain, lubricating the pathways and creating bridges between the neurons over the synapses, and *voila!* (#3 in Figure 3.2) the fact is allowed into the holy temple of long-term memory, the prefrontal cortex.

Whew! We're lucky that Alex had the sense to shake her head clear and do some things to help her brain to guide the fact into the correct place in her brain. She did a lot right. But it seems like she just stumbled onto the solution to her drama-induced and daydreaming problem. What strategies can we teach students to help them purposely shake off the daydreams and proactively attack a case of "having a tween moment?"

Tips for the Tween Brain to Learn Better

There's so much more that students can do to help their brains along when potentially stuck in the mires of high-wire emotion or the swampy doldrums of indifference. I've listed here a number of ways to help each step of the process and the part of the system that it helps the most in transmitting the message where it needs to go:

1. Stay healthy and get rest (RAS)

2. Take breaks and touch base with your emotional state (RAS)

3. Reflect to embed knowledge (amygdala and hippocampus)

4. Take breaks and switch modalities (amygdala)

5. Deep breathing (amygdala)

6. Review and practice (hippocampus)

7. Visualize yourself in a peaceful place (amygdala)

8. Laugh (releases dopamine)

9. Do some physical activity (releases dopamine)

10. Be kind to someone (releases dopamine)

Sure, all of these things are obvious, but it's the *why they work* that's so fascinating to students. Feed into this fascination and get those students working to increase their learning by understanding what makes themselves learn. Help them take ownership in their own learning.

Look, we all know that teachers can't do it alone, so give students the knowledge of how to improve and you will have created an ally in your battle against low achievement.

As you know, however, we also can't assume that it's totally up to them. The teacher also has to begin to design lessons with these strategies in mind.

Remember that because the prefrontal cortex is one of the last things to develop, tweens need adults to give them guidance in the structure and expectations of lessons. Therefore, if you can tap into some brain-enhancers in your lesson content and activities, you will have tapped into a gold mine of buy-in.

Teaching Brain-Centric Activities

1. **Yawning Before a Test**—I once read that Apolo Ono, the cute speed skater who also won *Dances with the Stars* (I admit it, I'm a watcher), always deliberately yawns before each race. It's not because he's bored or didn't have a good night's sleep. It's because he proactively loads up his brain and muscles with an extra oomph of oxygen to use in the final moments of a race. With a couple of deep yawns, he brings more O_2 into his system that he physically draws from when he needs it the most.

2. **Take "Syn-naps"**—Judy Willis states that allowing spontaneity is not just about engagement, but about literally waking up the brain. Along those lines, I sometimes follow a Twitter feed in my classroom (see Chapter 11 for more on using social media in the classroom). I specifically subscribe to kid-friendly news feeds or sites that pop up story starters onto our list of tweets so that while I'm teaching, something might pop up behind me that is interesting and we can stop, investigate, switch gears for a second, and then continue.

   For instance, I subscribe to Awesome Stories. This is a primary news footage site. One day, early in the year, I was discussing narratives and the concept of *setting* to my students and a tweet popped up on the feed that was the news footage and audio from the Hindenburg disaster. I stopped the lesson, we watched and listened to "Oh, the humanity!" and then I turned back to my students and had them open their Writers Notebooks and write about what they saw as it related to setting. It was a spontaneous switching of gears that woke them up and lubricated their neural pathways, allowing for greater engagement for a longer period of time.

3. **Rotating Seats**—I wrote about this in Chapter 2. What I want to mention here is that rotating seats isn't something that has to happen at the beginning or end of a class. In fact, in the middle of an activity (and I'm not saying this has to happen all the time or the disruption will be too much), why not say, "Oh, by the

way, can you put your pencils down, pick up your books, and move three desks to the left around the table?" The smiles and grumbles and eye rolls are enough to wake them up, and by the time they've seated again, there's some O_2 in the brain that wasn't there before.

4. **KWLH**—Sure I like the KWL (*Know-Want to Know-Learned*) chart as much as the next teacher, but what about adding an H at the end for *How did you learn it?* It asks, in a very simple way, for a student or class to reflect on the process they went through to learn a concept, and is a very nonthreatening mode toward deeper reflection.

5. **Let Them Drink Water**—Eric Jenson, the brain-based educator and author, encourages students to drink water during their learning process. It doesn't just wet the whistle; it also hydrates the brain and its functions. Dehydration affects the salt level in the blood, which upsets stress and blood pressure. The brain can phase out, get caught in the doldrums, and lose attention span. Therefore, let kids bring in their water bottles or fill them up at the fountain. It's good for them in many ways, but in this case, it actually creates greater awareness and alertness in the classroom to keep hydrated.

6. **Flash a Picture Between PowerPoint and Keynote Slides**—I love putting nonsequitur slides in my PowerPoints just to see who is paying attention. For instance, if we're flipping through slides of the translation of a Shakespeare monologue and there suddenly appears a photo of snowboarder Shawn White standing next to a cardboard cutout of werewolf hottie Taylor Lautner, I move on. The kids' heads whip up, shouting to "Go back! Go back, Mrs. W!" To which I reply, "What are you guys talking about? Now, let's get back to the couplet at the end." It's not only entertaining for them, but also for you.

7. **Instantaneous Think Aloud**—"Stop, drop, and write!" I yell. Suddenly, the tweens in the room drop to the floor, pens in hand while I pass out index cards to get a mental snapshot of what they think of what we're learning. It's a written Think Aloud of sorts, and an immediate reflection done in such a way that it wakes them up to do it. They never know when it's going to happen, and when they return to their seats, the O_2 is flowing for the next phase of the lesson. I can read the cards aloud or read them later at my leisure to reflect for myself on the lesson that I created and on my own teaching.

8. **Attach a Lesson or Unit to Music**—Each day as the students learn about Langston Hughes, have some jazz in the background. Each day as the students read about the Renaissance, have some strings playing on Pandora.com. Create an attachment to a concept that is nonlinguistic so that you can make it memorable before the RAS filter as a chance to toss the lesson aside.

So keep 'em moving, keep things spontaneous, and keep their brains active even while their bodies are stationed in their seats. The content isn't enough to do that. But specific, targeted, brain-based lessons can help.

Further Research

Here are some more resources that are fun to explore. Dip your toe into the pool, and just check out some interesting videos, books, and articles on the subject of the human brain and body.

- ◆ Eric Jenson, *Teaching with the Brain in Mind* (Alexandria, VA: ASCD Press, 2005)

- ◆ http://www.internet4classrooms.com

- ◆ http://www.radteach.com

- ◆ http://www.edutopia.org

- ◆ TedTalks: http://www.ted.com/talks/lang/eng/michael_merzenich_on_the_elastic_brain.html

- ◆ The Learning Channel: *The Teen Species* (video available on http://www.amazon.com)

- ◆ http://www.slimgoodbody.com

- ◆ Neuroscience for Kids: http://faculty.washington.edu/

- ◆ Steven Pinker, *The Language Instinct: How the Mind Creates Language* (New York: William Morrow, 1994)

- ◆ Steven Pinker, *The Stuff of Thought* (New York: Penguin, 2007)

4

Tips for Using Data Formatively

Follow effective action with quiet reflection. From the quiet reflection will come even more effective action.

— Peter F. Drucker

In Chapter 3, the students learned about their brains, because, as we've established, tweens love to learn about themselves. However, developing a tween-centric curriculum isn't just about supplementing your content with Easter eggs of tween-themed articles, factoids, or methods, it's also about helping students analyze themselves. To analyze themselves as they relate to your material, whatever the subject, requires that they examine the data that represents their learning.

The plan is for the students to use their assessments formatively by interacting with them beyond the actual event of taking the test itself. By doing so, the student will be further embedding the information into the prefrontal cortex (long-term memory) and will create a larger bank in the hippocampus to relate to new information as it comes in later on.

See the relationship?

To accomplish this, you need to use a routine trail of lessons that doesn't end at assessment taking, but rather, begins at the end of an assessment. This trail of targeted analyses and reflections should become a routine postassessment unit, with each segment of mini-lesson building into another. It all starts with tweens seeing themselves for whom they really are as learners, and it finally ends in achievement. This "lesson trail" of sorts can be unearthed when we learn the following:

♦ Why tweens need to look their data squarely in the eye

♦ Allowing for retakes

♦ Teaching tweens how to reflect on the data

♦ Teaching tweens how to set goals based on their reflection

♦ Sample Lesson Trails

By introducing your students to themselves, they will gain greater potential the minute you bring this additional reflective strand of knowledge and expectation into your classroom.

Why Tweens Need to Look Their Data Squarely in the Eye

It's important that tweens look at themselves in the academic mirror accurately. So much of their life is in flux that it's important that tweens are given concrete, indisputable evidence about who they are at this time as learners. An academic snapshot of sorts.

It's like going to a diet center and weighing in weekly. You don't just weigh in at the start of a year or quarter and go on your merry way until the following weigh-in at the end of the term. No. You look at the number, mull it over, and figure out if it was the milkshake or the chocolate cake that sunk your efforts. You go back, improve on some choices, and come back again to take another measurement of your effort and learnings. So is it for student achievement. A student takes an assessment, and reflects and learns from the test, then comes back to see who they are again.

Frankly, there is great power in tracking one's own data throughout the course of the school year or even through his or her entire middle school career. So I propose that each student should be given a file, digital or otherwise, at the start of middle school, that allows him or her to chart assessment scores on a graph for each subject matter. Students should own their own data, setting goals for themselves, and tracking their progress throughout the year.

You know which class already does this? Physical education. It's true. Students typically keep a file where they track the number of sit-ups, times it took to run the mile from week to week, pull-ups, etc. The rest of the classes should be taking a tip from PE and following suit.

Classroom teachers need to play a role in reintroducing students to themselves as learners. The students need to have their temperatures taken frequently and consistently to determine who they are now as students, not whom they were a moment ago, because in middle school, things can change rapidly. I had a student as both a seventh grader and an eighth grader. She was a great kid: tons of potential, athletic, well-spoken, great leader, funny, could work with anyone kindly. In seventh grade, she was making Bs with no problem. But by eighth grade, she had morphed into Perhaps-I'm-Really-A-Goth-Girl. She still had potential; she was still a kind kid and athletic and funny and all those other things. But with a boyfriend and some poor choices socially, she was making Cs and Ds without a whole lot of regret. School just wasn't the priority anymore. A certain percentage of the problem, the percentage I could help her with, had to do with her thinking she could keep her head above water as she had before. Some of the problem was that she just needed to look her data in the eye and stop deceiving herself that she could coast and still get those Bs.

The fact is, these kinds of kids are all over the place in middle school and are easy to catch because they are merely trying on costumes, sometimes at the expense of their grades. The good news is that these students can be caught in our achievement nets again by just bringing their data to their attention on a constant and consistent basis.

Allowing for Retakes

There is a power in allowing students the opportunity to make up, do over, and retake. Why not? If we are preparing them for the "real world," then how can we continue to argue the one-strike-and-you're-out rule? After all…

- Director William Wyler was reportedly known as "90-Take Wyler" for his use of the do over in many of his movies. Incidentally, he was the director of such films as *Ben-Hur, Roman Holiday*, and *Wuthering Heights*.

- To complete her Newbury Award-winning book, *The Single Shard*, Linda Sue Parks wrote more than thirty revised drafts.

- In a game of friendly or charitable golf, when you mess up a putt, a shouted "Mulligan!" will allow you the chance to try again.

So why is it that students can't retake tests or do certain questions over, having learned how to make them better? Robert Marzano talks about this very topic in his book, *Classroom Assessment & Grading that Work* (2006), where he challenges the idea of the one-stop assessment and instead offers suggestion of the power of retaking assessments to show evidence of eventual understanding.

Reward students for learning from their mistakes by allowing them opportunities to improve on their failures. Let them turn in late work, if it means the work quality will be better. We are pressed for time in the classroom and desperate for reteaching time. So we should reward students who take their free time to look at their missed standards and try to reteach themselves by working on skipped questions, rushed answers, and flubbed responses. It's the growth, the improvement, that is tantamount, not the initial grade.

Remember that our goal isn't to have some quota of failures in the class, but to give potential failures the opportunities to succeed; and for some students, that means working with them beyond the traditional timelines of testing and moving on. It means using assessments formatively. It means giving them the chance to make it up. It means allowing them the do over, the retake, the mulligan.

Teaching Tweens to Reflect on the Data

Imagine just how effective it would be to have students take a preassessment, score their work, chart their score onto a graph, and then reflect and articulate the reason for their answers. After all, education is not only about content but also about communication, and reflection plays a huge part in communicating intent.

It would be oh-so-easy to just sit down with a kid and say, "You answered A because you didn't read the question hard enough. It asked for '*not* the correct answer,' not which one '*was* the correct answer.'" But the power is in the student coming to that realization without you holding their hand.

So allow tweens to look at their lessons through their own unique lens. Give them reflection opportunities at the end of each assessment, and spiral your lessons so that they become a constant cycle of learning and reflecting. By teaching students how to reflect on the job that they did, they can learn from their weaknesses, and that is a future skill.

Some of this takes modeling your own reflection too. Think aloud yourself (see Chapter 6 for more on thinking aloud) and share your thoughts on whether a lesson went over well and why. Reflect publicly and you will find that your students will be more apt to reflect honestly and comfortable doing so. Did your most recent lesson on European trade routes during the Middle Ages stink so badly that it tanked in front of the kids? Verbally wonder aloud why. Why not ask your students why the lesson didn't work. Did everyone miss question #3 on the unit test? What standard did it cover? Ask them why it didn't stick. Better yet, ask your students what they think it would take to get processed into their long-term memory. (Hint: Just asking for their input might be enough to put it there.) By modeling your own comfort at reflection, you will create a culture comfortable with learning from mistakes.

> *By teaching a student how to reflect on the job that they did, they can learn from their weaknesses, and that is a future skill.*

A great and easy assessment tool for reflecting on your own classroom data as a teacher is www.surveymonkey.com. Surveymonkey collects the responses from all of those who took the assessment and compiles the data easily so that students can look at all of the responses, anonymously, and reflect on the meaning of the trends. In other words, Surveymonkey does all the hard work of a data technician for free. If you create a quiz in Surveymonkey's basic program and have the students click away at the answers, it will then collect all the responses and produce a chart for you to see all percentages of answers at a glance. What an easy way to assess a group.

Incidentally, it's just as easy for a student to create a practice assessment for other students to take using Surveymonkey. It brings them into the world of data collection, and regardless of your subject matter, incorporates a vital math skill into the classroom. In addition to an online survey tool, the students can reflect on their own discovered data using any number of offline methods, including:

1. Exit Cards

2. Thumbs Up, Thumbs Down

3. Essay

4. Rank Order Questions

5. Peer Interview

6. Dual-Entry Journal

So you've given them opportunities to reflect after looking at the results of their assessments, but you also need to give them the chance to record their thoughts and observations of themselves during their assessments.

When assessing, make sure you have copies of tests for students to take notes on as to what they were thinking at the time they chose the answer they did. Make sure you allow them to take notes *as* they are taking a test, not just in order to study for one. This allows them to go back to a test after it is scored to look at the snapshot of themselves as they took that test.

A tween is a sponge. This whole age group wants to learn how to do things better. They are just becoming aware of their place in the bigger world, and they want to be a big fish in a bigger pond. Teach them how to use their own brain, and then teach them how to dream of using it better.

Teaching Tweens How to Set Goals Based on Their Reflection

So a student has taken a test, seen his or her scores, and reflected on what it would take to do better. From here it's about students using that data to set future goals.

Maybe the goal is standards based. Maybe it's holistically based. Maybe it's personal. Whatever objective you set for them overall, by allowing tweens to set their own goals, graph their own improvement, and look back on their struggles and victories, you will give them further ownership in their own learning. By teaching them to set goals and objectives, you will have better overall buy-in, and individual goal setting is a key step in differentiation, which is an understandably huge challenge for many tween teachers.

I have been known to create constitutions with my class, setting goals for behavior and effort at the beginning of the year. We've practiced signatures, made quills, dipped them in ink, and signed them in our metaphorical blood, sweat, and tears. But there's no reason not to set goals in a less formal way periodically throughout the year based on the data as it presents itself.

Students can reassess their objectives using any number of methods, including:

1. Short-Answer Journal Entry

2. Color Coding a Data Graph with a new dot indicating where they want to be

3. Card taped to a desk as a reminder of a goal

4. Signature at the bottom of a statement of intent

5. A one-sentence statement in their weekly agenda

But analyzing data isn't just about your students setting goals; it's also about you, the teacher, setting goals. Using data formatively isn't just about students setting goals about what they need to learn, it's also used to help you set goals about what needs to be taught. After looking at the results of an assessment, it's valuable to break that test down into its components, and figure out your next steps.

Some programs do this for you. For instance, our district uses *Data Director*, which, despite its bugs as a test generator, is a great program for data analysis. All of our multiple-choice answers from our students get scanned into this program and it tells us what standards have been nailed and which ones are still missed by the majority of the students.

Next, once you've analyzed what the students know, this should help guide your teaching. Now, *Data Director* may be intended for adult use, but the real power is in showing students their own data from the program. They can see pie charts, bar graphs, and matrix tables on standards achieved and failed that are color coded to match from assessment to assessment. So for linguistic, nonlinguistic, or logical learners, *Data Director* holds great potential for setting them on the path of goal setting.

However, to help your students through their own process of data analysis, reflection, and goal setting, you need to specifically design targeted activities that ask it of them. The following section has a couple of examples of what I call "lesson trails" that do just that. These are concrete, day-to-day examples of how I help students to routinely involve themselves in the formative analysis process.

By designing lessons and routines that students know will happen at the end of each assessment, the resulting packets of "Lesson Trails" becomes evidence of learning. The packets become proof to parents, administrators, and the students themselves that learning is an ongoing process and that they are actively participating in that process in your class.

Sample Lesson Trails

Lesson Trails lead one after another, building toward a goal. We step onto one stepping stone, accomplish that task, then jump to the next one, which can only be tackled if the one before it is complete.

I find that learning from assessments, and using data formatively, is like stepping on those stones to the get to the riverside of comprehension; and I've developed routines of postassessment Lesson Trails that by second quarter or so become routine and expected by my students. For tweens, routines in the classroom are vital. It's a part of the importance of feeling in control, of feeling secure in their own learning, and feeling let into the secret of what it will take for them to achieve.

Depending on the format of what the students are being assessed on, you can develop a trail packet of sorts that makes the entire process transparent. By making the process transparent, you are also publicizing your own efforts as well as the efforts of your students (see Chapter 14 for more on this topic). I've included here a description for two different kinds of Lesson Trail packets: one for formatively reflecting on essay writing, and one for formatively reflecting on a multiple-choice assessment of any subject.

Lesson Trail Packet for a Written Assessment

For my tweens to learn from their writing assessments even after they've turned them in, I set up a process of continued interaction with the essay through a series of activities, even after the timed writing is done. What they end up creating are really messy, superbly worn-in packets that track their thought process through the entire writing process. The end-result packet is not pretty; but neither is thinking. It includes the following:

1. **The Original Assessment**—The timed writing is, in actuality, a rough draft. Given only sixty minutes to read a story and write a five-paragraph literary analysis on a simplistic tale is most likely not going to produce a fantastic essay, to say the least. Sure I give this a score; I have to, right? But I also design an additional score that shows growth, and this initial assessment becomes the rough draft on which we begin our writing journey.

2. **Peer Revision Packet**—Peers read each other's essays and help to give feedback to the author (see Chapter 7 for more information). The rough draft (what was once the final assessment) now has a beaten up look about it, complete with author and peer revision sticky notes, crossouts, scribbles, and arrows to new or

improved passages. The messier the better. The essay itself has been tossed out of the bar with some black eyes, and told to never come back until it is of a better quality. Nevertheless, this draft is never thrown out. It becomes a part of the Writing Packet to show how far the writing has grown.

3. **Revised Draft**—The author takes all the marks and advice into consideration and writes or types up a clean draft.

4. **Own Your Own Feedback Sheet with Self-Score Card**—The author then meets with me for verbal feedback (see Chapter 12 for more details and an example of my feedback sheet). By being the one to take notes on the feedback, the students own their learning. By filling out what grade they believe they should get based on the feedback from the meeting, the students also decide then and there whether to go back to the drawing board on certain issues. This is a form of formative goal setting.

5. **Final Draft**—If the students believe that there are further revisions or edits that need to be made, they turn in a final draft (handwritten or typed) to be included in the Writing Packet.

6. **Student-Translated Rubric**—(See Chapter 7 for an example of a student-created rubric.) The students switch or rotate essays so they can be scored by a peer on a student-created rubric that has been translated from the standard district rubric. The author also scores his or her own essay. Finally, I score the final essay on the same rubric so that the student can see where I agree and where I disagree with the students in our feedback.

7. **Writing Reflection Statement**—The students then complete a reflection sheet on the process, answering questions about specific improvements that they made throughout the writing journey. First created by my colleague and fellow Writing Project member, Liz Harrington, I have tweaked its design to have students direct their reflection to indicate the differences between edits and revisions. Figure 4.1 (page 48) is my version of the template.

8. **Goal-Setting Statement**—Finally, the students set goals for future essays using an index card. On one side are the lessons learned, and on the other side are the goals they still want to achieve.

Figure 4.1. Template for a Writing Reflection Statement

Writing Reflection Statement

Author Name: _____

Essay Title: _____

After you have revised and rewritten your paper, look back at your previous draft(s) and at the comments you received. In the chart below, describe in detail what you did to improve your writing in the most recent, final draft. An example has been provided for you.

Editing Changes	Revision Changes
Paragraph #1—added an "s" to the end of "jump" to make it agree with the subject.	I switched around the sentences in the second paragraph, making the main topic sentence the supporting sentence. I used a two-word sentence to add suspense in my third paragraph.

The most important changes I made were: _____

_____

_____

_____

_____

_____

_____

Based on the rubric, I think my paper should score a _____ for the following three main reasons:

_____

_____

_____

The entire packet is stapled together in order (original assessment on the bottom, goal-setting statement on top) and put into the student's portfolio. After all, I'm not just interested in what their best work is throughout the school year; I want to see the work it took to produce that work.

At Open House, those packets come out and sit on the desks, and although they may not look the neatest or tidiest, anyone inside or outside of education can see the work that went into creating the final drafts.

Lesson Trail Packet for a Multiple-Choice Assessment

Inspired by my colleagues Kenna McRae, Liz Harrington, and English Language Development teacher Linh Phuong, I now use a Formative Assessments Folder for each student. This folder, which can be used for any subject, becomes a yearlong vault of information for a student that is a concrete resource for them to analyze his or her own growth. In May, it doubles as a test preparation folder for standardized tests. However, if it were just test preparation, then it would be only a vessel for our multiple-choice assessments that students could use as study guides. It's how each student interacts with his or her individual test preparation folder after he or she takes the initial assessments that makes it formative.

Basically, each student gets a folder. You can have them decorate the outside with symbols of test taking for a nonlinguistic spin if you want. Depending on the assessment being analyzed, the packets therein could look something like this:

1. **A Copy of the Assessment Questions**—Let's say this is the packet of fifty questions that they used to take the initial test. When taking the test, the students should be encouraged to write in the margins, highlight words in the passages, etc., to show what they were thinking at the time they came up with their answers. I also say this at the time of the test: "Please circle your answer in the test booklet prior to bubbling in the response on your scantron."

    I know this might sound tedious, but let me illustrate why it is necessary. Later, when we're looking at the scantron and trying to see what we got wrong, the student can look at the response they *meant* to bubble. Nine out of ten times, I'll hear something like, "Wait a minute! I circled B, but I bubbled C. Argh! I bubbled wrong!"

    It is a concrete way to analyze a simple fact: Even the best middle school students make bubbling errors. It's a fine-motor skills issue. One year, I even had an Honors student realize that he had made six bubbling errors on a single assessment. However, he was able to look his carelessness in the face, and couldn't argue his mistake.

By getting the additional information that the circled response gives them, the student can decide for him- or herself whether it was a careless error or a lack of content knowledge.

2. **The Original Bubble Answer Sheet They Filled in**—This way they can't dispute how they answered or the accuracy of the actual scantron machine.

3. **Reflection Chart and Short-Answer Packet**—This is a two-page sheet that asks students to analyze why they missed certain questions, what words they may not have understood, and why the correct answer on the score sheet is correct. Once again, based on Liz Harrington's original sheet, Figure 4.2 is my template for the Multiple-Choice Reflection Packet.

4. **Goal-Setting Statement**—This can be anything from an index card to a more formal writing piece. What are their goals for next time? Are they going to work harder to show understanding of a certain standard or are they setting a percentage goal for themselves in how they will improve from Below to Proficient by moving up 10% in their correct responses?

Data Displays

In the end, regardless of the format of the test, students should be creating data displays for the room to advertise the improvement of the class as a whole.

Eventually, you can give them the data that represents their class from the first quarter: How many students scored Advanced, Proficient, Basic, Below Basic, Far Below Basic? By fourth quarter, give them the stats again and have them create graphs to show overall improvement.

This allows those who might still be below, but who have improved, to feel celebrated, even if the scores are anonymous; and for those who have not improved, it can open up a dialogue between you and them about why they have remained immobile for ten months while others have managed to move toward proficiency, even if only slightly.

Regardless, by the end of the year, through analyzing their own data and being brought into their own assessment process, more students will improve. I've seen it. Using data formatively is vital for tweens because it gives them control in their own accomplishments.

Celebrating their growth visually and audibly gives them a sense of victory even in the face of challenges to come. Figure 4.3 (page 52) provides examples of data displays.

Figure 4.2. Multiple-Choice Reflection Packet Template

What score did you get? _____

How many problems did you get right? _____

How many did you answer incorrectly? _____

How many bubbling errors did you make? _____

How many errors did you make because you didn't understand a word in the question? _____

Please create a list of words or phrases that challenged you on your multiple-choice assessment:

_____   _____

_____   _____

_____   _____

Of the questions you answered incorrectly, please reflect on the following:

#	Your Response	Correct Response	Why You Chose What You Did & Why the Correct Answer Is Right
5	A	B	I chose A because I thought it was asking for the character trait, not the main idea. It's actually B because the author wanted the reader to understand that we are dependent on the environment's health to survive.
5	C	A	I chose C because I read the question too quickly. It's A because when you move the X over to the other side of the equation, you get ¾.

Figure 4.3. Examples of Data Display

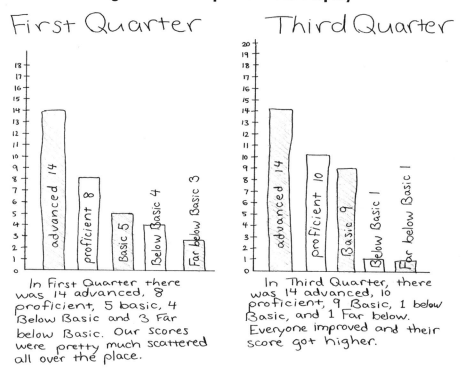

First Quarter

advanced 14
proficient 8
Basic 5
Below Basic 4
Far below Basic 3

In First Quarter there was 14 advanced, 8 proficient, 5 basic, 4 Below Basic and 3 Far below Basic. Our scores were pretty much scattered all over the place.

Third Quarter

advanced 14
proficient 10
Basic 9
Below Basic 1
Far below Basic 1

In Third Quarter, there was 14 advanced, 10 proficient, 9 Basic, 1 below Basic, and 1 Far below. Everyone improved and their score got higher.

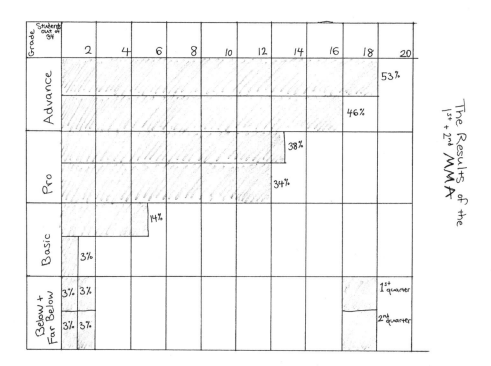

The Results of the 1st + 2nd MMA

5

Tips to Help Keep Their Time Meaningful

One thing you can't recycle is wasted time.
— Author Unknown

Yawning. Notes being passed. The occasional muttered comment said under the breath for everyone near to hear. No, I'm not talking about the faculty in an afterschool meeting, I'm talking about middle schoolers. Bored ones.

Bottom line, the most powerful tool in tween classroom management is to avoid having bored middle schoolers, and the best way to avoid the spreading of texting, the vacant expressions, and the eventual discipline problems is to make their time meaningful in your classroom. Just because it appears in a textbook, does not mean that tweens will understand the value a concept will have in their future lives. You know, honestly, just between you and me, not everything we've been told we have to teach has the same level of value, so we need to prioritize what's important so our students don't attempt to do it for us.

This takes four steps, all of which are covered in this chapter in these topics:

- ♦ Talking to your students about why they have to learn a skill

- ♦ Teaching tweens how to be skeptical appropriately

- ♦ Predicting what skills tweens really need to have in the future

- ♦ Making lessons applicable

The first and most simple step in making sure a tween's time is well spent in your classroom is to be upfront with them. Let them in to the truth of what's important and why. Now, I'm not the type of teacher who says things like, "kids these days…!" But the fact is that kids these days *are* busy; they *are* savvy; and they *do* deserve an explanation as to why school and lessons are important. If you show them the respect of explaining why they have to learn a lesson, and if you take a little time to share how it applies or will apply to their lives, then they will pay you back with greater buy-in, which leads to a more successful class.

It's not engagement through entertainment; it's engagement through being pertinent—and an engaged class is easier to teach.

Talking to Your Students About Why They Have to Learn a Skill

"Why do we have to learn this?"
"Where does this appear in the real world?"

We've all heard this before. In fact, I may have been the tween that asked you. Frankly, I never did get a good answer. I wonder, though, why isn't school considered the real world? The fact is that there's been this huge disconnect between what we do during our K-12 years and what we do in the years beyond, and this has done teachers, professionally, a great disservice. The key is in connecting the dots.

The way to combat this disconnect is, as Bloom's Taxonomy says, to *Apply*. Make the lessons connect to their lives now by teaching them skills that will enable them as future contributors to their world.

The difficulty comes when the story in the core curriculum you *have* to teach is making even *you* drool with boredom, or the concept they have to learn in the math book you know will *never* be seen again. It's hard to prove to students how something will apply if you yourself can't see why it's necessary. It's true that education is peppered with nonapplicable directives—What career needs to know how to bubble?

When a tween asks why something is necessary, we can't respond "because it's in the book," "because it's on the test," or "because the standards say so." We don't get off so easily.

There are other stock answers I've developed that I actually use when I'm at a loss. So when a tween asks, "Why do we need to learn this stuff?" here are some possible responses:

1. "Well, what may mean nothing to you, may have great impact on that kid over there. That's the beauty of differentiation."

2. "You never know what your future holds, and what may mean nothing now, may be a vital lesson for later."

3. "It adds to your toolbox of background knowledge. You may meet someone one day and it might end up being something you can connect with."

4. "Hey, a true Renaissance person learns it all, OK?!"

And there's another answer I give that requires a little more to it. When asked by a student how this lesson or that lesson could possibly help them later on, I have been known to say the following:

> OK, think of it like this, and this is a metaphor: Our brain is a muscle and like any muscle in your body, it needs to be worked out before you can do any heavy lifting. Learning is kind of like that. Different lessons develop and build up different parts of your brain. That's why we learn about so many different things. Math hits one muscle, science and history hit other muscles, electives hit muscles. This is so your brain develops in a more well-rounded way so that when you're ready to pick what you want to do in life, you've got tools in many categories to help you make that choice.

You have to teach them to be skeptical with style.

Be prepared, however, because some tweens still may not buy it. Consequently, you have to teach them to be skeptical with style; if you can eliminate the eye roll, it's bound to improve your daily tween experience.

Teaching Tweens How to Be Skeptical Appropriately

Middle schoolers have places to go and people to see, and you want your classroom to be on that agenda. Just as they are frightened that the party will be going on without them, they are also frightened of being left out of the know. They are suspicious of the other truths that they suspect might be going on underneath the surface of what's being told to them. It's called skepticism, and that's a great thing to have, and it's developmentally appropriate for them to have it.

So don't squash their natural skepticism; use it. Don't hate that they challenge everything; teach them how to challenge appropriately. Don't fight their need to test boundaries; teach them how to test them. Don't be frustrated by their need to question; teach them how to question. In the end, when they realize that you are in their corner, preparing them honestly for their lives beyond school, they won't be bored, they won't be difficult. They'll be listening and participating, ready to learn.

We also must remind ourselves that these tweens straddle two worlds: the world of the ready and the world of the not-really-ready. They are no longer in elementary school where authority is, for the most part, something more eagerly followed, but they don't yet have the skills of the older student to question authority without an eye roll thrown in.

When teaching students how to question appropriately, it's important that the students realize that those who stand against them aren't "crazy."

Teachers, for instance, aren't on the other side of the fence, just shaking the students' cages because it's fun to tease the animals. Students must learn to show their middle-school-level disagreements or skepticism with a certain grace or they won't be treated to the level of answer that they feel they deserve.

I always use this example:

> OK, say you want to stay out past curfew. Do you yell and scream for your mom to let you, and when she says, "No way!," do you call her nuts? Does that ultimately help you? Of course not. But, what if you were to give your case calmly and acknowledge you understand where she's coming from? You'd at least be more likely to hear the answer you want, right?

It's all about being civil, and it's all about learning that we're all here for the identical goal: their achievement. If they want to challenge you, at least teach them the common booby traps of arguing poorly.

To address this, I've provided a handout (Figure 5.1) of some argument pitfalls that tweens (and arguably some adults) should be aware of when constructing a written or oral argument; and arguing is what many tweens do, so help them to do it well. Besides, tweens love knowing the real names of things, and it's all about using content-level vocabulary yourself so that they begin to use it too. These represent what I believe to be the most often used argument traps that ensnare our tweens.

Figure 5.1. Typical Argument Traps

- **Argument to the Man (*Ad Hominem*)**—attacking the person rather than the point

- **Argument of Generalization**—attacking a whole group

- **Needling**—poking at your opponent simply to make them mad

- **Scare Tactics**—freaking out your audience with scary scenarios as a means to make a point

- **Generalization**—assuming what's generally true must always be true

- **Oversimplification**—boiling the topic down too much

- **Appeal to Vehemence**—just being plain loud or yelling over your opponent

- **Cyclical Reasoning**—your argument is used as its own proof

- **Cliché**—using the slogan on a bumper sticker as proof

- **Bandwagon**—because so many people do it, or did it, it must be good evidence

- **Pigheadedness**—just plain-old stubborn

- **Non Sequitur**—what?! The dots are not connected

- **Error of Fact**—warning: one error generally means there are others. An audience loses faith in the author when they hear a factual error

- **Failure to State**—taking no side or wavering in your position

- **Uninformed Opinion**—there's no evidence. The debater doesn't back up their opinion with fact

- **Two Wrongs Make a Right**—just because one side did it does not justify that the other side should

If students really want to know how something applies, teach them how to research its application: Who does a job like this as a career? Where else does this skill exist? Help them channel their suspicious nature into a superpower, and you will create better trust in what you are teaching.

Of course, questioning the *why* something is important is only a part of how to make their time meaningful. The other key as a teacher is to try to make sure that as many lessons as possible are authentic and important to learn.

Predict What Skills Tweens Really Need to Have in the Future

"Why do we have to learn this?" We've heard this from our students many times before, and to answer this question, I'm going to first ask you to do a little math:

> Enter the grade you teach _____ + the number of years until your students graduate from college _____. Add this number to the year you find yourself reading this book. The resulting year = _____.

So what does the world of that graduating class look like? Does it look the same as the one you faced when you graduated college? Of course not.

It's hard not to teach as we were taught, but that's not our job. Our job is to prepare our students for their futures, not the future that once was. Studies show that there are new skills and new abilities that these kids must know in order to compete in their future. Now, these skills don't have to combat our required standards; they are, however, the methods in which we should teach them.

Sometimes, however, these methods may seem at odds with what parents (or even some fellow teachers) think should be taught. But ritual and tradition aren't good enough reasons to continue teaching a certain skill or lesson. Remember that a lesson must be meaningful for a student to really excel, and "that's why we've always done it" is never a good enough reason.

In fact, there are numerous skills that students must have to function in life as their future selves. And when I find myself slipping into teaching something or functioning in some ways "just because," I refer to the following three resources to remind myself of my goals:

♦ **Did You Know?**—Go to YouTube. Type in this title and watch the most recent version you can find. It's just a simple iMovie with a powerful message about the future of education in this country, using up-to-date data about America's education system and the international systems at large. Created by Karl Fisch and Scott McLeod, it's made the rounds of every professional development I've ever been to, but it's worth watching it repeatedly for a reminder of how to make our teaching relevant.

♦ **Guy Kawasaki**—I've been following Guy on Twitter for a while now. He's an Apple Fellow and an entrepreneur who educates me in a way that trickles down to my students. If you want a really inspirational read, find his "Hindsight" speech that he gave in 1995 to Palo Alto High School. (It's even been known to occasionally find its way into my students' hands.)

♦ **Mr. Winkle Wakes**—This short animated film by Matthew Needleman is a quick, eye-opening, funny take on what happens when old Rip wakes up to find life having changed around him...except the schools. I find Needleman's www.creatinglifelonglearners.com a great resource in digital storytelling as well.

You also need to think about how to prioritize the many standards out there. Many schools have adopted "essential standards" to indicate the power list that the department believes carry the most importance. Familiarize yourself with your school's essential standards, but keep in mind that these too may not be as necessary as some neglected skills. For instance, if you watch educator Arthur Benjamin's speech on www.Ted.com, you will see that he makes a case for why math classes should be focusing more on probability and less on the mathematics and algebra that lead up to calculus. He makes the argument that probability is far more practical and essential when one eventually leaves the school environment.

However, I believe that there are cross-curricular skills that students need, independent of individual subject area standards. Therefore, based on my own research, here is a list of thirteen skills that I believe students really need to learn. Create lessons that teach them or create activities that use them as a means to incorporate them into your students' academic diet. It will help students connect with your material, and will help make your lessons more meaningful.

1. **Collaboration**—Learn how to work in groups. It's a given in the business world and has become a given in our global community.

2. **Communication**—Learn how to talk to anybody at a party. Learn how to speak with respect to both the waitress and the owner of the restaurant. Learn how to talk to your boss and your coworkers. Learn how to write an e-mail, leave a voicemail, even shake a hand. Learn to read the communication of gestures and expressions, and understand what your gestures and expressions send out as well.

3. **Problem Solving**—Learn how to research answers and solutions. Learn where to go and how to get there.

4. **Decision Making**—Learn how to be definitive.

5. **Understanding Bias**—Learn how to recognize agendas.

6. **Leadership**—Learn how to be a leader, not a ruler.

7. **Questioning**—Learn to be skeptical appropriately (see above section), to question with clarity, and to inquire calmly. Learn to question as a means to guide others to an answer, and learn how to use questioning as a means to make your own knowledge deeper.

8. **Independent Learning**—Learn to find answers yourself.

9. **Compromise**—Learn to find contentment even while giving something up. Learn to find contentment by finding a middle ground.

10. **Summarizing**—Learn to get to the point.

11. **Sharing the Air**—Learn to shut up. Learn that you can learn from others.

12. **Persuasion**—Learn the art of persuasion both in the written and spoken word.

13. **Goal Setting**—learn to define your quarry and hunt it down. Learn to identify and visualize where you want to get to and the path that can get you there.

We've been to our educational past and seen our educational future, but now I want to give you some ideas with how to handle your present.

Making Lessons Applicable

Nothing on the above list clashes with current philosophies of teaching or the standards movement. However, contrary to what has become our reality, standards were only meant to be a basic foundation and universal language in our education system, *not* the ultimate ceiling in our students' learning. Just because a lesson is standards-based does not miraculously make it applicable to our students' lives. Therefore, we have to use them to serve as a guide to focus our lessons so that they can resonate more with our students, making the time spent in school more relevant. In fact, the relevancy of a lesson can be presented in the content, the delivery, or even the assessment.

Below are some examples of ways to include relevancy into your lessons, allowing your students to inject more of themselves into their learning. It creates more buy-in, after all, and a student who is "with you" is more likely to learn.

1. **Ask Questions at the Start of a Unit**—For instance, before reading Langston Hughes' "Thank You, Ma'am," I once asked my seventh-grade class the question, "Have any of you ever stolen anything?" Now, I'm not saying I loved what I heard, but they listened to the story after our discussion.

2. **Involve Primary Sources**—Let's say an eighth grade history class studies the Constitution. A teacher could bring in a copy of his or her own teacher contract or a copy of the student handbook or online student permission slip. Perhaps it could be a homework assignment to ask an adult about a contract that they have had to sign, its purpose, and its effectiveness.

3. **Bring in a Guest Speaker**—I once knew an eighth grade science class that was studying DNA. During the unit, the teacher called a forensics expert buddy of his to come talk to his students about his job, his knowledge of DNA, and its use in solving crime. Contact your local board of education, PTA, Elk's Lodge, or other civic group for networks of people outside of the school to tap. Pull those strings with your own group of friends, and you'll find lots of folks willing to come in and share their expertise with the students.

4. **Use Project-Based Learning**—PBL, a book in itself, has the student develop an authentic goal that requires authentic skills in which to achieve it. For instance, a sixth grade class learns to write a persuasive essay. They could come to a consensus as a class and write a persuasive letter to the principal and the board of education asking for a particular elective to be offered the following year.

The following is another example of project-based learning that my own class has been involved in and the skills that are being covered as a result of the unit:

Our new school bell is terrible. I mean it's this synthesized Big Ben wannabe chime that we hear no less than twenty times a day. Furthermore, it's unsynchronized; that is, it functions like a rolling earthquake in that it rings first in one wing of the school and then makes its way down campus in an echo-like roll of Casioesque horror.

My students decided to take matters into their own hands and use persuasive writing to beg the powers that be to change our bell. It just so happens that the new computer routers for the school are located in the back of my room and the new bell is housed in the mounted big black box. Therefore, when the maintenance crew came in one day for something, I simply asked, "Hey, is there a choice of bells up there?" They foolishly said yes, and thus began a persuasive writing unit of project-based learning. As I write this, there is a petition being organized as evidence, a committee of letter writers working on our thesis, our proposal, our counterargument, and call to action, with a panel of students readying an oral statement to be read for the principal and vice principal to get our diabolical bell changed and synchronized. The kids found the goal, and they're using their skills to try to solve the problem.

Skills used and taught: collaboration, communication, problem-solving, independent learning, and goal-setting

To develop your own project-based learning unit, check out Edutopia. org's Project-Based Learning summer boot camp. Also check out the following books for your own PBL professional development:

- Suzie Boss, Jane Krauss, and Leslie Conery, *Reinventing Project-Based Learning: Your Field Guide to Real-World Projects in the Digital Age* (Eugene, OR: ISTE, 2008)

- Phil Schlemmer, M.Ed., and Dori Schlemmer, *Teaching Beyond the Test: Differentiated Project-Based Learning in a Standards-Based Age, Grades 6 & Up* (Minneapolis, MN: Free Spirit, 2008)

Regardless of the scope of your objective, the lesson must resonate with the middle schooler for it to really work. The bottom line is this: If you don't know why you're teaching something or assigning something, I challenge you to do something daring…don't use it.

6

Tips for Teaching Deeper Thinking

Thought flows in terms of stories—stories about events, stories about people, and stories about intentions and achievements. The best teachers are the best storytellers. We learn in the form of stories.

— Frank Smith

Did you ever see Kevin Costner's film, *Dances with Wolves*? Remember that wolf that tentatively skirted around the outside of the soldier's camp, searching for attention? Remember how many times we had to sit through seeing Costner try to coax that wolf toward him to eat from his hand? Well, getting a tween to share their thoughts, to make connections to their content, is kind of like that. We have to coax them. Not with beef jerky, but with your own thoughts and commentary. Then you'll have them eating from your hand, and when they begin to listen to the hand that feeds them, they will begin to learn how to think for themselves.

Our thoughts and commentary must occasionally come from our own archive of anecdotes. Middle schoolers are like toddlers in that they will drop everything to listen to a great story. Telling stories shares with them your thinking process as you went through life. Children aren't born knowing how to make decisions. Students don't just appear having learned how to problem solve. You have to model it for them, and middle schoolers, who are notorious for thinking more about their nonacademic world than their academic one, will more likely respond to lessons hidden in the anecdotes of your outside life than those stated on some poster hanging in your room or stated in some entry form the textbook. Additionally, telling stories fills in the blanks between obvious ideas, willing in the dark matter with the thinking that when on between your decision making.

It is the start of Think Aloud, a process many elementary teachers use faithfully, yet an all-important process underused by those of us in the secondary levels.

Sharing your own stories promotes an honesty of thought in the classroom, and honesty disarms a tween and makes them more susceptible to learning. As a result, they will begin to open up their minds more cognitively, and that is an honesty of thinking that you can use to help them improve their achievement.

Sharing selected and purposeful parts of your past and present is the best way for your students to learn how to succeed as a learner. Now, I don't mean you need to share so much that you invite your 250 students over for Thanksgiving dinner, but I do mean you should tell them about how to cook a turkey. Better yet, share how you once burned the bird and ended up making a Stouffer's lasagna. Thus, you've modeled both flexibility and the ability to problem solve while laughing at yourself.

If the content is the A story, then the Think Aloud is the B story traveling alongside the curriculum. This constant B-story of curriculum, this buzz of storytelling that underlies your content, creates a relationship with your students. What you share models your own thought process, and from that base you can train students to exploit their own stories, thoughts, and musings to help create a deeper understanding with the subject matter. This chapter discusses the following concepts:

♦ You are the supplemental material in your classroom

♦ A cautionary word

♦ Creating a classroom culture of Think Aloud

♦ Helping students merge their lives and their learning

Share stories. Model honestly. Use yourself and your life as an example. Think Aloud. Model your own struggles as a learner. Yep, I said it. Fess up to them. Admit as a teacher there may have been challenges you had as a student. I know I did. I start honestly sharing from day one. No joke.

You Are the Supplemental Material in Your Classroom

I start the year promoting a culture of storytelling. Stories are, after all, where commentary and original thought spring from. And when I say "start the year," I mean from the very first day. Sure the first few days of school are all about routines and rituals, how-tos, and where things are. But I also make time to start the deeper learning through an activity called "Find a Fib."

Find a Fib

I saw educator and author Erick Gordon present a version of this activity during my summer with the California Writing Project. He used it to begin writing memoirs with his students, but I use it as an opening-day activity for two purposes: building community and beginning the thinking aloud and modeling culture that is the cornerstone of my classroom.

The game begins by presenting the class with a list of factoids about me. Ten of them are facts and one is a fib. The object is to guess the fib. With each one guessed that is, in fact, true, I get one minute to tell the story of that bullet point. Thus, I can easily segue into memoir or narrative writing if I should choose, which was the point of Gordon's initial presentation.

For me, the true point of the discussion is to get someone to guess the fib. When they hit the fib, well, then I start a little verbal memoir.

Here's my list of factoids:

1. My father is the 1969 World Champion Jeopardy player.

2. I was kicked out of Brownies in fourth grade.

3. When I was a child, I was a model on *The Price is Right*.

4. When I was fourteen, I went to Greece and dropped my coolest pair of sunglasses into a well of frogs.

5. My dad was one of the creators of Capt. Jack Sparrow.

6. When I studied at Oxford University in England, I ended up having an emergency appendectomy.

7. My husband and I met in second grade.

8. My mother and I are both certified scuba divers.

9. When I was in school, I was a straight A student.

10. I once worked at a guest ranch, working in the stables, leading the kiddie rides across the Arizona desert.

11. One weekend, I was so bored that I went skydiving just to do something new.

So, did you guess the fib?

That's right: # 9. So begins a little subliminal soapbox number, because you see, I was definitely *not* a straight A student. In fact, I was far from it. In some classes, I was what I call now an "easy B," that is, I got a B with no problem. The fact is that I really wasn't interested in doing anything more than what it took to get that. For other classes, I struggled to get Bs, Cs, and even scored the occasional D. Truth be told, I didn't find a joy in school or in learning until I found subjects I was interested in, ones I could choose myself and lose myself in, the occasional high school and college class.

The important thing, I tell my students, was I kept my academic head above water enough so that doors weren't closed to me. By not limiting the open doors, I could sample enough to find a passion in life. I admit to them that it shocked the heck out of me when I discovered it was teaching.

So why is it important to share this particular story right off the bat? Because our job isn't to just reel in the students who already love school and are good at it. Our job is to reach those kids who don't love it yet, who aren't good at it yet, but who still have the potential to discover learning. That's why I love middle school. Every kid in middle school still has that potential, even if they seem to be going down a dark path. Every kid is still able to be lead down another path, and sometimes the path we see as dark lightens up a bit in time. Frankly, even if they appear to be heading down the seemingly "right" path, tweens can still wander off at any moment. Therefore, as teachers, our nets need to be superwide to catch as many students as we can.

> *Our job isn't to just reel in the students who already love school and are good at it. Our job is to reach those kids who don't love it yet... but who still have the potential to discover learning.*

You are the supplemental material. Your stories fill a chink in the achievement gap. Mind you, it may be a little chink, but hear me out on this one. Tweens are notoriously disinterested in much of what goes on outside their little world. So parents and teachers must specifically target filling this knowledge gap, the gap of what's happening outside tweendom, if we are to begin pushing students to be able to make connections and commentary based on the greater world around them.

I see it every day. For instance, every Monday morning, I open up the classroom at 7:30 AM for kids to hang out in, get warm in, and check out a book. In that time, I learn a lot about my students, and the fact is that some kids just come back from their weekends having, well, lived more than when I last saw them.

This supplemental education, provided by their families and other adults, started from birth for some of the kids, and continues as a parallel road of education. Maybe it's going to museums. Maybe it's going camping. Maybe it's helping to build the deck. Who knows, but it is adult-guided time where a student is learning while living.

But what happens to those students who don't live an outside life, who aren't receiving this additional education that seems like such a vital component in their achievement? Where is their supplemental learning coming from? The answer is: you. Put aside the philosophical greater issue here of whether or not it is our job to provide what families are not. The fact is that our job is to teach. Bottom line: If by sharing my outside-of-school experiences with my students can help bridge that divide somehow, then I will.

It doesn't take much. Let's say we're reading Langston Hughes' "Thank You, Ma'am." Maybe the class walks in that day and I'm playing an Elvis song. Maybe I hack YouTube and show a clip of Denzel Washington reciting Hughes' "I, Too" from "The Great Debaters." Maybe I pull the class outside and show them how to play stoopball the way my own dad showed me how they did it growing up in the New York streets.

You must bring the authenticity of the outside world in. You must invite them to relate to school through you, because they may not have any other way to connect to education.

A Cautionary Word

Notice, however, that I'm only talking about selected stories of your past. That's because as a teacher, as I'm sure you know, you must be careful about what you share. The whole embarrassing-picture-of-yourself-at-eighteen-posted-on-Facebook-issue is still up for debate about whether you should be held responsible for it now, but there's no debate that a questionable story shared in the classroom about your past behavior or vices puts you directly in the line of fire. Use the power of storytelling wisely and it will also model to your students a higher standard of storytelling. Be smart. Be the adult in the room.

Make sure you follow some guidelines, however, when you are sharing stories of your past or present:

1. **Don't share anything you wouldn't tell a person to their face—** When I teach persuasive debate and counterargument, I always conduct a lesson where the students first think about an issue that they are irked by with someone, and have to role play their opponent's arguments to see the opponent's point of view. I always choose to share the fact that my husband and I fight over the TV remote. It's benign, but the tweens love to hear me argue myself. The point is, I don't mind if my husband knows I'm sharing this particular thorn in our sides.

2. **Be smart**—They don't need to know everything you did in college. Surely you can find another example from somewhere in your life to model the lesson of not doing what the masses tell you besides that asinine moment where you learned the hard way not to jump off a roof into a pool.

3. **Make sure that your anecdote connects to the material**—Non sequiturs are no fun, and students will know if you just like to hear yourself talk. I used to have a high school teacher who drifted in and out of the curriculum, sharing tales, and then returning to the book for no reason other than to muse. Finally, a frustrated student created a sign that sat in the back of the class that read "DRIFT!" in big letters, so that whenever the teacher

drifted off-topic, the student would flash the sign and reel her back in.

4. **Make sure your story has a message**—We don't have instructional time to waste. Let your students know that even their lives have themes; they just need to pay attention to their own tales. It's that additional level of curriculum that we, as role models ourselves, must find opportunity to supply.

The next step is to ask them to begin to make their own connections between their prior knowledge, even their present experiences, and their classroom learning. If they begin to do this, they will think less and less of school life as functioning separately from real life. Before the merging between school and the outside world begins, however, these stories must move beyond listening to your own tales, and become a more integrated part of their own participation in the classroom. These stories must become sniper-like Think Alouds that are constant connections to the material.

Creating a Classroom Culture of Think Aloud

How many times have you asked, "What are you thinking about?" only to hear the disappointing answer, "Nothing"?

Have you ever asked a student what they learned in class yesterday? What's their answer? "Nothing."

How about when you ask if there are any questions? Silence. Crickets, in fact. Translation: "Nothing."

But it's not possible. Their brains are always on, always working, always questioning, always relating. More often than not, these students just don't know how to express or retrieve the fleeting thought that they have, and that's where you come in, modeling your own stories, your own Think Aloud.

I've always thought of Think Aloud as a tickertape that goes through my brain, much like the news while you're standing at a deli counter. Our experiences, our stories, our prior knowledge all create this conga line of connections that travel through your brain at breakneck speed with each piece of input received.

Metacognition is the act of thinking about thinking, and it's the tickertape in your head that never ceases. It's the captions underneath your living movie. It's the voice over going on at all times while life trudges ever onward. Most kids don't even know it's there.

It's up to teachers to model how to pause the tickertape, analyze it, capture it, articulate it, and even reflect back as to how that thought came to be in your head.

It's up to teachers to model how to pause the tickertape, analyze it, capture it, articulate it, and even reflect back as to how that thought came to be in your head. This ability, however, goes against everything that a middle schooler stands for. They are transparent, yet they don't want to share what's inside.

Being able to freeze that tickertape, read it, and use it to make connections to our material is a powerful tool that we must model and actively teach. Think Aloud and modeling are important arrows in the quiver that each of us brings to the classroom. Each teacher comes with his or her own valuable variety of arrows, and if we all use them, our students will have a variety of supplemental material in which to pull from in addition to their own. Therefore, whether you are a new teacher fresh out of school, a veteran with years of life and school experience, or a second-career teacher with knowledge of what else lies beyond, you have unique tickertapes to freeze and share. In so doing, you will help our students freeze and utilize their own.

As I've said before, Think Aloud is one of those strategies that are used often by elementary grade teachers, but seems to drop off our secondary teachers' radar as a targeted strategy to use. What you must remember, however, is that in middle school, you have an unlimited supply of tools. Many that work in both elementary and high school might work with the tweens in front of you. Think Aloud is one of them.

Teacher-poet Taylor Mali said it best in his poem, "What Teachers Make," when he bragged that teachers have the power to make students, "Show all their work in math/And hide it on their final drafts in English." However, to do either of those things, show or hide, takes knowledge of what got you there in the first place, your thought process. Teachers must help students recognize their explosion of neurons that are firing at all times in their brains like Fourth of July at the Hollywood Bowl.

Think Aloud is a strategy that can be used for reading anything from a story to a word problem to an article on any subject matter. Connections are possible regardless of the genre. For teachers, it can be fairly easy to simply freeze the tape and find the valuable connection to a piece of writing. For many learners new to the strategy, however, think aloud requires a scaffolded approach.

Rather than simply asking them to freeze and give you their immediate response, for which you could risk hearing that they are thinking about lunch or the end of the period, provide for them a guided list of connections to think about. For instance, in my class we talk often about using the following steps when using Think Aloud during our reading:

1. Activating Prior Knowledge—What does this remind you of?

2. Determining Purpose—What is the intent behind these words?

3. Making Connections: World, Media—Does this event or moment make you recall anything from the outside world beyond school?

4. Predicting—What can you guess happens as a result of this moment?

5. Visualizing—What are you picturing right now?

6. Asking Questions—What does this make you want to know more about?

7. Monitoring for Understanding/Summarizing—Can we put this in your own words?

8. Applying What You've Learned—How does this apply to the topic we just discussed in class?

Once the students get the hang of it, however, do not demand the scaffold; they will find connections all by themselves. The effectiveness is in the modeling of thinking in real time rather than the requirement of assigning a student to complete these strategies in a given text.

For instance, prior to assigning a Writer's Notebook entry I might sit down in front of the class with the document camera all set up and my own journal on the desk. Maybe my prompt is "My History as a Reader," a prompt I began using when my current district adopted a very powerful writing program called America's Choice. I'll begin by writing my own paragraph first, but I'll be talking about my decision-making process as I write: Why am I choosing this word over that one? Why do I like this sentence pattern? Why am I crossing out this thought even though it's a rough draft? etc.

Figure 6.1 (page 70) is an example of one such entry. The handwritten lines are what my students saw, and I've provided speech bubbles of what they heard me sharing as I wrote. Each revision and edit represents a thought and each thought I verbalized for the class.

The goal is to be messy. After all, thinking is a messy business. Thinking is always a rough draft. Whether you teach Language Arts or math, history or science, sharing *your* thought process will help your students recognize *their* own thought process.

Helping Students Merge Their Lives and Their Learning

You've laid the groundwork by storytelling and establishing a Think Aloud culture, one of tickertapes and snapshots. Now how does this translate to student success? Sure, it's easy to share about me, but now the trick is to pull original thought from them, and teach them when to use those thoughts to create deeper work.

Figure 6.1. Think Aloud with Writing

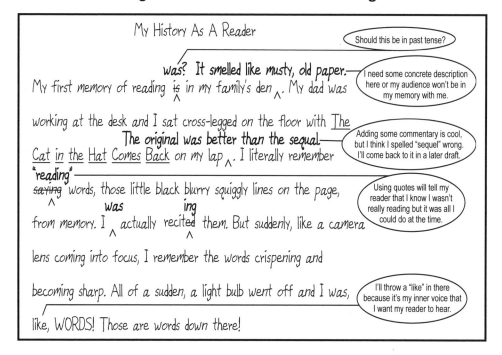

To address this overarching goal, as the year unfolds I do more than just narrate while I work. I very pointedly have my students do metacognitive exercises so as to build up their ability to freeze their thinking tickertape to give them tools for their own writing and comprehension. What follows are a few activities to coax the original thought from the tween brain.

Quickdraw with Student Scribe

I first learned this activity from Carol Booth Olson, the director of my Writing Project branch. She is the author of *The Reading/Writing Connection* and she does this activity with clay for a three-dimensional model. I've modified it to include the use of the computer, starting off with a two-dimensional doodle before advancing to more advanced Think Aloud brain/communication exercises later in the year.

Step 1. Prime the creative juices by going onto Stefan J. Bucher's *The Daily Monster* website at http://344design.typepad.com/. This blog is by a designer who basically creates movies of himself doodling a squiggle that then develops into a monster, complete with a little narrative.

Step 2. Pair the students up and number them as 1s and 2s. The number 1s are the artists and get a piece of drawing paper and a crayon. The number 2s are the reporters and get out a piece of lined paper and a pen or pencil.

Step 3. Set a timer for only a couple of minutes, and allow the 1s to draw a squiggle, having them develop it into their own monster like the Bucher piece you modeled earlier. As they draw, they should narrate their thought process. For instance, here's a ramble I overheard during one such activity:

"OK, so here I am drawing this beak-like thing. It's pretty long. Maybe my monster's related to a toucan. You know? That thing on the cereal box? Anyway, maybe it doesn't have wings, but it has wheels. Maybe it's a robot monster and some scientist got carried away with his recycled parts or something. I made a bird-feeder once in second grade from a recycled milk box thing…"

Meanwhile, the number 2s are taking notes on what's being said. They shouldn't worry about getting all the transitions down, just the main beats of what's coming out of their partner's mouths.

Step 4. At the end of the time, the recorders show what they heard from the artists, who generally don't remember saying all of it, so it's basically a surprise to them. What it amounts to, however, is Think Aloud. Figure 6.2 (page 72) is a more visual example of the activity.

If you were to categorize some of what was said in the above example, you could see elements of real, albeit odd, metacognition here in the form of Questioning, Connection to Self, and Connection to World. The goal here is to create activities that promote Think Aloud, that work out their brain in tickertape activities so that they can learn to access thoughts at the drop of a hat.

If this were, in a sense, a rough draft of an essay about this monster, this student could refer to the cartoon as evidence; and by looking at these bizarre notes, they could perhaps flush out deeper word choice and connective themes, change it to the more omnipotent third person, and thus, create a paragraph of higher-level commentary based on the initial Think Aloud.

These kind of activities, conducted on a frequent basis, result in the level of writing you can see at the end of this chapter with my student's example from the story, "Both Sides of the Fence."

Figure 6.2. Student Quickdraw

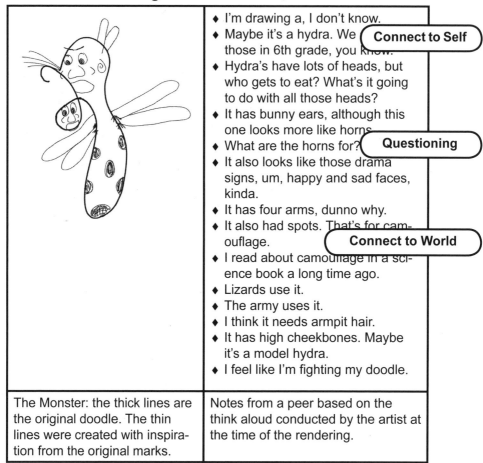

The Monster: the thick lines are the original doodle. The thin lines were created with inspiration from the original marks.	Notes from a peer based on the think aloud conducted by the artist at the time of the rendering.

Dual-Entry Journals

♦ **Language Arts:** Another very basic brain activity is to have the students look at political cartoons or text and create a dual-entry journal that basically reflects What they See (Evidence) vs. What they Think About (Commentary). The students read the excerpt from a work of literature and can create a bulleted list of textual evidence. On the other side of the chart is what their own brains think about the text that enhances their knowledge of the subject of the writing.

♦ **History:** Have students look at primary resources, like political cartoons, and create a dual-entry journal of evidence (what actually appears in the document) and commentary (what connections they can make from accessing their prior knowledge of history or current events.)

◆ **Science:** Have students look at a picture from nature, say, a particularly dramatic weather pattern from space or watch David Bolinsky's Ted.com video of cell animation. In their dual-entry journal, the students take notes on what they see. This is their Evidence. Their Commentary would be their predictions or connections of the deeper meaning behind the images.

◆ **Math:** Give the students an overly elaborate equation, perhaps one that is just above their heads. In one column, let the students dissect the equation in any order they wish, to recognize the components that they do know. These components are Evidence of what they know. In the opposite column, have them explain what they recognize. This is the Commentary. See how far the kids can get to solve the equation or recognize what the equation is for. It's OK if they can't solve it (although that would be the ultimate goal). However, their own compartmentalized analysis might show you what they *do* know and might lead them to deeper thinking about the subject and equation overall.

Now, to really develop a culture of Think Aloud and help the students merge their lives with their learning, you can't merely do these kinds of activities once and expect the results of deeper awareness of thought. After all, just as you can't go to the gym once, work out your glut once, and expect a firm derrière, you can't just do one activity that activates Think Aloud and expect a deeper thinker. If your modeling and sharing isn't constant and honest, then their willingness to "go there" for you won't reveal itself.

Remember the wolf from the movie that needed to be coaxed out of its shell. Tweens are like that wolf. They need to be given something in order to give of themselves, and their trust, their knowledge, and their commentary need to be coaxed from them as well.

I want to end this chapter with the results of my efforts in storytelling and Think Aloud in my Language Arts class. Eventually, students put these lessons of Evidence and Commentary together into a Literary Analysis. By training students to build up their ability to be *aware* of their tickertape, you will pull out deeper commentary in the end.

Here is a paragraph from my student Johnny's Literary Analysis Benchmark of the story "Both Sides of the Fence" *before* Think Aloud strategies were taught:

"Alberto's tree grows over to Juan's side of the fence and Alberto doesn't like that. That leads him to the mayor. 'The next morning,

Alberto returned to the mayor and presented what he imagined to be Juan's side of the case.' He thinks he knows Juan's side."

By the end of the semester, after doing countless Think Aloud activities and sharing throughout the year, coupled with lessons on transition words and phrases, I had the students revisit their benchmarks to revise. Here is the end (*after*) result:

"The reader learns that Alberto's tree grows over to Juan's side of the fence and Alberto doesn't like that. That leads him to visit the mayor. In fact, the rising action of the story builds when, 'The next morning, Alberto returned to the mayor and presented what he imagined to be Juan's side of the case.' The misunderstanding is an example of the conflict and shows that Alberto only thinks he knows Juan's side. There is always another side of a story to think about, even if you are angry. This theme actually appears in other stories too. For instance, in 'The War of the Wall,' the two boys learn that what they thought about the painter lady proved untrue. In 'Both Sides of the Fence,' Alberto is like those boys misunderstanding Juan who could also be the painter lady. If we all just walked up and asked each other what they really meant, wouldn't many problems go away or never even start? The character (and I) learn that talking solves a lot."

Tap into your stories, your background knowledge, and thinking process verbally, and you will be modeling how students can tap into their own brain as well. Teach them to freeze their tickertape and be aware of their own deeper thinking. By using these all-important strategies, a student can provide deeper commentary in any class, will have more ownership in his or her own learning, and will see a greater meaning in school's relationship to his or her outside life.

7

Tips for Teaching Tweens to be Teachers

Teaching is the highest form of understanding.
— Aristotle

Tweens think they know everything. But don't blame them. Being an authority is how a tween begins to learn how they want to define themselves. Tweens glom on to a skill or an ability, and want nothing more than to be an expert in that one thing. It's the reason why all tweens seem to be obsessive about something. Maybe that student is an expert in an entire book series, like Rick Riorden's *The Lightning Thief*, Stephenie Meyers' *Twilight*, or J.K. Rowling's *Harry Potter*. Maybe the student is an expert Rubik's Cube figure-outer or Magyck the Gathering card player. Maybe the student is great at drawing Manga. Maybe the tween is a great writer or math student, skateboarder, or 100-meter sprinter. And then there are those tweens who are expert procrastinators or sleepers. It almost doesn't matter what is the subject of expertise, because with every student obsession can be found a teacher possibility.

So I say go with it. Teachers must tap into their students' need to be experts by training them to take their obsession one step further. Students must be taught to teach. They must learn to teach each other, and in so doing, will learn to teach themselves. After all, education's job is not to always be there for the student, but to give them the skills to be their own source of education during their life. What a tragic classroom it would be if the students always remained the pupils.

Don't get concerned that the role of the teacher is totally being passed off here. I am not suggesting we use students to teach instead of teachers, but rather to encourage their ability to use certain qualities found in teaching.

Think about the skills a teacher needs to do his or her job. Here's a partial list:

1. Communication

2. Research

3. Problem solving

4. Setting rigorous expectations

5. Giving feedback

These are the skills of not only a teacher, but of a leader, of a group member, and of a key player. Skills that students will use in their own futures. Someone once said that "Teaching is the profession that teaches all the other professions," so why not sow the seed of teaching early on?

The key to teaching students *how to teach* is to scaffold mini-lessons throughout the year that lead up to a culminating unit called *Teach the Teacher*. The mini-lessons pepper throughout your regular lessons, use your regular classroom content, and focus on reinforcing teaching abilities. I'm going to break it down for you as follows:

- Students teaching students
- Reinforcing teaching skills
- Speaking an academic language in the classroom
- Student-created rubrics
- Student-created assessments
- Teaching the Teacher unit

Students Teaching Students

We all know that those who are doing the teaching are really doing the learning. In other words, those who are communicating the content are really embedding the information into their long-term memories. Consequently, it becomes very important to remind ourselves that it's not us who need to be doing the communicating, it's the students.

Communication in a classroom comes in the form of teaching and guiding, so we need to train students to help guide each other. By helping each other, it will, as a grand result, also become embedded into their own minds when they are asked to work independently.

I might call it peer teaching to them, but between you and me it's really self-teaching.

See? Sneaky. I might call it peer teaching to them, but between you and me it's really self-teaching. From working with their peers—teaching, discussing, communicating, and advising—students will take their own advice back to their own desks and practice what they've been preaching. You'll see the results in their buy-in, and you'll also see the results in their assessments. After all, we cannot ignore the need to do well on tests. Frankly, there's nothing I'm advising you to do that doesn't help toward that goal. Just think about it in regard to parenting.

For example, I have been known in my life to be a rather messy person. If I'm being forgiving, I like to say that my bedroom is a picture of my brain. It somehow makes it more romantic. A more objective person, however, would just tell me it's plain ol' messy. Now, it is not a goal of mine to raise a messy toddler, so I am always telling my son to put his books on the shelves, his toys in the bins, and his dirty clothes in the laundry basket. Do you know what has happened as a result? I've become more organized myself. It isn't just about modeling. It's about reinforcing the lesson and the natural osmosis that occurs when you are a teacher or, in my case, also a parent.

Now apply it to the classroom. When a student is paired with another, catches their mistakes, and explains why it's a mistake and how to solve the problem, it encourages the students' own ability to use that skill. Teaching reinforces skills. But how do we make sure that students are reinforcing the correct skills? That's where you, some scaffolding, and some targeted activities come in.

Reinforcing Teaching Skills

Regardless of your subject matter, students can be teaching students; this isn't somehow scapegoat teaching. There are those who bristle at the thought of students somehow advising other students, as if this is in lieu of any guidance from the actual teacher in the room. This couldn't be farther from the truth. In fact, teaching students to teach each other requires great teaching skill on your part, and if they can communicate successfully, it becomes an assessment for them.

Don't be scared away from trying some of these strategies. You won't be working any harder; rather, you will be working more efficiently. The other by-product is that you'll have more fun as a teacher. Greater student achievement and more fun for you in your job. What do you have to lose?

1. **Revision Stations**—In 2008, I was lucky enough to hear Writing Project Fellow Maureen Rippa speak about using Revision Stations in the writing classroom. In a nutshell, each table in the classroom becomes a station with a purpose, many of which allow students to teach each other after I've initially taught the lesson or unit to the class previously. When you think about it, it isn't so much teaching as having students reinforce and role-play as teachers. Although I learned stations that had a Language Arts focus, the fact is that stations can be designed for any number of subjects or tasks. For instance:

   • *A math station might* focus on the logic used in a word problem. At this table, students read each other's word problems and use sticky notes with guided questions on them to encourage the author to revisit his or her thinking or writing quality.

- *A technology station might* be focused on test preparation. As I discuss in Chapter 11, I use Twitter on occasion in my classroom. This station consists of a computer hooked up to the LCD projector, set up with the classroom Twitter account already open. Here students post onto Twitter any reflection they have based on test prep strategies. This can be the mistakes they've discovered, some great advice they want to share, a eureka moment, etc., but it can also be a question they have. Another student from class can respond when they wander to the station or, better yet, if another class that follows us has its account open at the same time, a student from another classroom or school site might answer the question posed by my student right on the spot.

- *A language arts station might* use a peer review packet as a means to convey advice between two students. Here a student sits down with peer, exchanges rough drafts, and fills out a review packet of activities that is based on the genre being written. For instance, the packet might include the following activities:

  - Write another hook for their peer

  - Create a word splat of high-level words, a word bank created by a peer looking to identify great vocabulary

  - Keep a tally of the transition words or phrases the peer has used

  - Indicate where the thesis statement might be in need of help

  - Color code different elements of the essay to visually display what might be missing from the paper

By filling out the packet, not only is a student reading an essay in a very targeted way, and commenting on it, but that student is also aware of how his peer might be responding to his own essay as well. In so doing, it makes a student aware of his own essay's needs when the student gets the paper back for formal revision.

By the way, the use of a peer review packet is universal.

- In math, a peer review packet can be created that breaks down the components of an equation, asking students to analyze different variables or a peer's process of achieving an answer. The stations could be very similar to those listed above in that they could help students answer lengthy analytical or word problems.

- In science, they could be used for lab work, breaking down the elements of the scientific method and verifying the accuracy of conclusions.

- In history, a student can have his history day project critiqued by a peer prior to finalizing it.

- In study skills, a station can focus on note-taking advice or binder organization.

Training these students to achieve as teachers gives them the highest-level communication skills ever. Additionally, there is also an awesome by-product. If you train them to be rigorous in their feedback of one another, they can be giving more individual attention to each other than you with your red pen ever could.

- *A cross-curricular station might* be a place for a student to ask for help regardless of his or her subject matter. This is the station where a student sits down and asks for help in that which he or she finds him- or herself the most weak. It requires a student to know enough already to be able to reflect on his or her own subject-matter weaknesses. It's the ultimate in student choice. For instance, a student might know that she is missing commentary in her literary analysis essay because the peer review packet told her so. The student can sit down at the Ask for Help station and specifically target that skill by seeking help from another student. (Generally, I hover in this area as a teacher.) My belief is that if a student has the ability to ask a question about her own weaknesses, then that student has given the lesson a great deal of thought.

Revision stations are the ultimate in differentiation. Eventually, something begins to happen even with those students who generally find themselves as the ones always doing the work in small groups; the fluidity of revision groups allows even these students to seek out others who are great at certain skills. By seeking experts themselves, by sitting down and listening to what these students have to say, students who generally help others are able to enjoy the act of learning from others. And just as watching a student teach is an assessment, so is watching a student listen and learn.

2. **Topic Tables**—Another way to go with students teaching students is to designate long, banquet-like tables in the classroom that focus on a given standard or topic. The adult teacher decides which students make up each long table. This can be based on what the students are still struggling with, what they already excel at, or what they have chosen based on a particular interest. The group can come to a consensus as to which student or students are the teachers of the group. (See Chapter 2 for more on how to build consensus in a small group.)

These student teachers are not unlike row monitors you might assign in a computer lab to be the first "go-to" students to answer questions before the questions get thrown to you.

These tables allow different students to work together with the goal of achieving something they may not have understood yet. The expert student is there to answer questions first, but what it really allows you to do is differentiate the classroom based on a chosen topic or missed standard. You can walk around answering the second tier of questions, those that can't be answered by other students. You can work one-on-one with students who need more attention or remediation. Meanwhile, the groups are working on their targeted activity, one that uses the strengths within that group, to tackle problems in a first wave of attack. In so doing, you are enabling students to solve problems by taking a step back in your own authority. Just as we do with our own children as parents, sometimes must we do with our students: give them the chance to think for themselves or seek out answers, with the security that you are there, in the background, waiting to catch them if they fall.

3. **Student-Contributed Content**—At every available opportunity, allow the students to bring in what will become the content of the lesson.

- When my students were studying persuasive word choice, they brought in products that used advertising slogans on their boxes. By having some ownership over the content, the students had more buy-in to the lesson itself.

- When I want students to pick the topic we are studying for the day, I have them bring in golden lines from their independent reading book, a line that really drew their attention, and speak about what they like about that line that made them pick it to share. Both Jeff Anderson and Kelly Gallagher speak about the power of the golden line, and they have both influenced my classroom with this strategy. What gets brought in is what drives the content of the lesson. For instance, if a student brings in a line, even one that might make your own eyes roll, that she loved from Stefanie Meyer's *New Moon*, you can use it to help drive that day's content. Let's say our Twihard fan brings in the following line:

"Before you, Bella, my life was like a moonless night. Very dark, but there were stars—points of light and reason....And then you shot across my sky like a meteor."—Edward Cullen

It seems obvious to me that what we have here is a jumping off point for a simile lesson. In fact, you can even begin the lesson by asking the student what she liked about the line. Undoubtedly, she will focus on the comparison, and that's how you will find yourself in a class with the student actually doing the teaching.

The power of using golden lines doesn't have to stop in reading or writing lessons. A student can bring in golden lines from any textbook for any subject. Perhaps a student finds a stated hypothesis very interesting that she found in her science book, an equation in a math book, or a moment in time from her history text. All a teacher has to do is recognize a teachable moment and ask the questions of the students that allow their voice to be heard more often.

- When you want students to make connections between what you are teaching and the outside world, have them chronicle a finding. If you are teaching about 45-degree angles, have them take a digital photo of one from outside school and e-mail it to you. If you are teaching about nimbus clouds or about the setting of stories, have them pick up a digital camera or their cell phone, snap a photo (with their parents' permission) and send it to you for evidence of an assignment well done.

4. **Student-Contributed Research**—Every year, across the country, students write the standard research paper. Generally, it seems that they are expected to research in a vacuum, all by themselves. But in the past, I have provided space in my room for a student-created research library of sorts that is built up of the resources that kids find as they conduct their own research.

Perhaps they find an article, bring it in, and put it in a labeled manila file. I have them include an icon, a symbol, a picture that represents the topic. It is then hung, face forward on the wall for the duration of the project's unit. No matter the subject, you can provide a location of accessible files of information brought in by the students.

5. **Online and Offline Discussions**—Allowing students to talk about topics prior to sharing them with the whole class, gives them authority to speak aloud and gives the input of fellow students the priority of the teaching. In other words, rather than a teacher introducing a topic and immediately jumping in to teach that topic by providing answers and solutions, it is more valuable to throw out a scenario and have the small groups discuss or debate the possibilities themselves. See what they can come with.

You can begin any class, in any subject with…

- "What would happen if…?"
- "Have you ever…?"
- "Where have you seen…?
- "According to _____, studies have shown _____. When has this been/not been true?"

The possibilities are endless, so allow the students to confer with each other, giving authority to their opinions and giving them opportunity to explain their points of view.

Once you have established the routine of conversation, debate, and dialogue, you can move into online formats of discussion. After all, discussion etiquette offline sets the level of discussion netiquette online.

Online communications, through blogs or threaded discussions, are ways for the students to continue teaching each other even after the school bell has rung. My colleague, Liz Harrington, a Fellow of the California Writing Project, was inspired by Allen Webb's and Robert Rozema's book, *Literature and the Web*, which prompted her to begin using threaded discussions in 2008. These online conversations, like blogs, are a way for teachers to just throw out a topic to her online class, and allow students to jump into an online conversation, creating a discussion beast all their own.

But this concept of allowing students to discuss and problem solve together first before the voice of the teacher is heard is a powerful one. When I asked Harrington why it's so important to allow tweens to discuss and talk amongst themselves, she replied (and make sure you read this in your head in a Scottish accent; Liz is a Scot):

> When students interact, whether face-to-face or in writing, over a text, they experience an increased ownership of the text. They find that they have to organize their thoughts more coherently so that their peers will understand what they are saying, and that this need for coherence is increased by the immediacy of the discussion....In addition, the reciprocal nature of discussion means that students also have to be willing and prepared to revise their thinking on the spot, and to consider the views of others in a very immediate and tangible way.

Teach the students to have conversations at an academic level, and their ability to develop a more academic voice in their own heads will grow. (See below for more on this topic.)

6. **Job Rotations**—In my language arts classroom, by the second quarter of school, I rarely set my colored pen to a student essay to show editing mistakes. Instead, I train my students to do it. Early in the year, I conduct mini-lessons on different convention skills: sentence combining, spelling, agreement, usage, etc., then I teach the students to teach each other.

So let's say a student brings in a piece of homework of some kind. They sit in their small groups and our job rotations begin. The rotate their assignments to the left with each job completion. Each student is focused on one task at a time. The first time the student reads a peer's work, their job is to solely be on the lookout for one kind of error. Then we rotate. Then the students are only searching for a different kind of error. Then we rotate again. Perhaps in the third round, the students are seeking out a particular skill to praise. This way you aren't always having them focus on the negative. Rotate, and so on. The jobs are based on the skills we've learned already. So, once again, I'm not handing over the actual teaching, so much as handing over the reinforcing.

Regardless of the subject matter, start by breaking down your own content into concepts. After you've taught lessons on each of the concepts, assessed students, and spent some time improving on their craft in that topic, then assign students to role play the master in each of the categories.

For instance, in science class the teacher gives the students an overarching guided question, "Hermit crabs will choose colorful shells over dull-colored ones," and the students each create a lab report using the scientific method. Each small group can rotate its completed lab report, seeking advice from their fellow scientists with each rotation. With each rotation of a student's essay, a student becomes a new expert in that category. Like this:

Student A passes his report to student B, student B to C, etc. In that first rotation, the students are looking only at the quality of questions that were developed as a first step in the scientific method. There should be a rubric (designed of course by the students; see below for instructions on how to develop a student-created rubric) differentiating between low- and high-level questions.

Then the students rotate again, this time becoming experts in what a great hypothesis statement would look like. Again, they are only looking at this one element of the lab report and giving feedback to their fellow student on that single element.

In the next rotation, the student is evaluating the quality of the observation notes or sketches. Rotate again to have the students evaluate their peer's analysis of their findings. Perhaps for the final segment of the scientific method, the one that focuses on communicating the results of the experiment, there can be an oral presentation. Students can use an oral presentation rubric (student developed, of course) to score each other as each student in the small group stands up to present a one-minute oral presentation about his or her findings.

Allowing them to instruct each other is all about communication and conversation, so it becomes important at this point to mention that you must teach students how to speak if you are going to let them speak together. What I mean is that you must use an academic language in the classroom to set the level of conversation.

Speaking an Academic Language in the Classroom

Don't mistake tweens for younger kids by allowing them to brush off rigorous words or content-level vocabulary just because some of them choose to suck on candy pacifiers. Similarly, don't assume that they are adults, able to be left alone to talk responsibly with no guidance. Instead, talk to them using the words of our profession. It helps with test taking, and it helps in how you relate to your students. We also can't assume that students know how to talk, to critique, to praise. Give them the sentence stems for debate and discussion and you'll have given them the tools to communicate in an academic setting and beyond.

Quick. Define the word *analyze*. Can't do it? Well, neither can most students. In fact, many teachers forget that the unique language of testing has to be not only translated, but also used often. After all, you might be taught a foreign language from a textbook, but if you aren't using it regularly, you won't remember the language. Case in point: I took Spanish from third through twelfth grade, and to this day I only remember the word, *lechuga*. That's right—lettuce.

To help you use an academic language in the classroom, I've provided a word cloud (Figure 7.1) of the oft-used words in standardized testing. The more you use them yourself in the classroom, the more you'll begin to hear students using them in their own conversations with one another. In the beginning, make a game of it, giving points for overhearing their correct usage. Remember that usage = embedding.

Figure 7.1. Word Cloud of Testing Terms

I chose to show you the words in a word cloud because visualizing the frequency of these words on standardized tests may have a greater impact on some students than the typical word list. To create such a cloud, cut and paste a list of words into a template at www.wordle.net. In this case, I compiled multiple lists of high-frequency, standardized test words and input them all into the field provided. What emerged is a visual of the most-used words.

Here's another way to determine the most important content-themed vocabulary to be using in the classroom. Cut and paste your content's state standards into wordle and see what picture is born. Figure 7.2 is a word cloud of the California English-Language Arts standards.

Figure 7.2. Word Cloud of California English-Language Arts Standards

In the spirit of students being teachers, perhaps the students themselves could input the standards, print out their resulting word cloud, and find ways to assess the frequency with which they use them daily or weekly.

Model your own usage, and reward them for using these words properly and often. In so doing, you will be giving them a tool in their own ability to communicate, and to communicate well.

Student-Created Rubrics

I use rubrics because I'm a big believer in not keeping secrets from students. I show them what I expect of them ahead of time. I show them how they are going to be scored before their assessment begins.

Many educators agree. For instance, I spoke to Anthony Cody, National Board Certified Teacher, member of the Teacher Leaders Network, and edublogger, about this very topic. He says:

> I actively experimented with giving more feedback to my students, using rubrics, models of student work, and having students assess their own work as well as that of their peers. This really transformed my teaching. I began to see the value of having a clear set of goals in mind when I began a unit. I could see how much more the students learned when I was clear about these goals....

I agree that using rubrics helps students set goals before and even during their assessments. However, as time passed, how I used rubrics changed from my early teaching days. Years ago, I would show my students the district rubric of a writing genre. I thought I was very progressive. I mean, by showing them the rubric used to score them, they could use it as they wrote as a guide to what we scorers needed to see. Right? Wrong! They never even glanced the rubric's way after I passed it out.

I'd preteach. We'd go through the expectations line by line, defining the words. Words such as *analyze, evaluate*, and *interpret*. However, I soon learned that, much like what Charlie Brown heard in the classroom, the language of the rubric and their definitions soon became a wall of nasally *whah-whah-whah*, losing the meaning.

I realized that while I saw the value in using rubrics and using all the teacherese, academic language in the classroom, it required translation of a different sort for the students to actually see their value too. So I asked myself, *Who could translate the rubrics in a way that the requirements could stick to the students' brains?* Ah! The students themselves.

So here's how you begin: First, you have to have the traditional rubric in front of each student. Figure 7.3 (page 88–93) is my district's rubric on writing a persuasive essay.

As you can see, it's pretty standards-based and aligned to the state rubrics. It's got all the qualifications of what makes a great persuasive essay, except it's boring, and with tweens, if it's boring, it's all over.

Now, starting with the numbers above, have the students (whether it's as a whole class, small group, etc…) translate what it means in their own words to get a 5, a 4, a 3, and so on.

I generally only interject my classroom monarch card once when it comes to rubric translation. I insist that the highest score should be described as "Able to Teach this Topic." Let's face it, if every opportunity to learn begins with the phrase "I don't know," then every assessment of having learned should begin with "Let me teach you what I know," and if what Aristotle says is true, that "Teaching is the highest form of understanding," then should not the "Ability to Teach" be our highest form of praise for a student?

Putting the "Able to Teach this Topic" at the top of an assessment rubric serves two purposes: first, it truly assesses students in their ability to communicate, a skill that is underrated in this era of testing but which will be vital to their futures beyond school. Second, it brings a respect for teaching into the classroom, and that's not a bad thing. "Able to Teach" should be the acme of A grades, and by defining the highest grade in a phrase form rather than a letter, students can better understand their goal.

> *Should not the "Ability to Teach" be our highest form of praise for a student?*

Go through each row of expectations, creating a gradation of accomplishment in their tweenese rubric. Figure 7.4 (page 90–95) shows how my seventh grade fared in its own rubric translation.

Figure 7.3. District Persuasive Essay Rubric

ELA ✚	Score 5 EXCEEDS	Score 4 MEETS
Ideas and Development	The response: • States a clear position. • Authoritatively defends position with precise/relevant evidence. • Convincingly addresses the readers' concerns.	The response: • States a general position. • Adequately defends position with relevant evidence. • Generally addresses the readers' concerns.
Organization and Focus	• Illustrates a clear, logical organization of ideas. • Maintains a consistent focus. • Clearly addresses all parts of the writing prompt.	• Illustrates a mostly logical organization of ideas. • Maintains a mostly consistent focus. • Adequately addresses the prompt.
Word Choice, Sentences, and Paragraphs	• Exhibits use of precise, sophisticated & descriptive vocabulary. • Provides a wide and effective variety of sentence types. • Includes highly effective use of transitions. • Demonstrates effective use of multiple paragraph construction.	• Exhibits use of some precise & descriptive vocabulary. • Provides some variety of sentence types. • Includes generally effective use of transitions. • Demonstrates adequate use of multiple paragraph construction.
Grammar, Usage, Mechanics and Spelling	• Contains few, if any, errors in the conventions of the English language. • Errors do not impede the understanding of the writing.	• Contains some errors in the conventions of the English language. • Errors do not impede the understanding of the writing.

Score 3 APPROACHING	Score 2 DOES NOT MEET	Score 1 FAR BELOW
The response: • Weakly states a position. • Defends position with little or weak evidence. • May not address the readers' concerns.	The response: • May not state a position. • Fails to defend a position with any evidence. • Fails to address the readers' concerns.	Illegible, no response, inaccurate response, or responds in a language other than English.
• Illustrates some organization of ideas. • Has an inconsistent focus. • Weakly attempts to address the prompt.	• Little or no organization is apparent. • Lacks any type of focus. • Does not address the prompt.	
• Exhibits use of mostly simplistic (basic and elementary) vocabulary. • Provides a limited variety of sentence types. • May include ineffective or awkward transitions. • Demonstrates weak use of multiple paragraph construction.	• Exhibits consistent use of simplistic (basic & elementary) vocabulary, and/or needless repetition. • Uses mostly short, simple sentences, and/or makes frequent errors in sentence construction. • Does not use transitions. • Demonstrates little or no use of multiple paragraph construction.	
• Contains numerous errors in the conventions of the English language. • Errors impede the under standing of the writing.	• Contains many serious errors in the conventions of the English language. • Errors seriously impede the understanding of the writing.	

Figure 7.4. Student-Created Persuasive Essay Rubric

ELA?	Score 5 ABLE TO TEACH	Score 4 IT GETS THERE
Ideas (What thoughts went into it)	• Great thesis statement that's a map of the essay. • Great evidence, quotes. • Great counterargument that says, "OK, I get that there are others who don't agree with me and WHY."	• Good thesis that says what you're going to prove. • Good evidence (quotes, personal experience). • Says there are people who don't agree, but don't give them a lot of time, space to explain WHY.
Organization (Can your reader follow it?)	• Really clear, like building blocks from one idea to another. • Bull's-eye everytime! • Every piece of the prompt is included clearly.	• The reader can definitely follow the logic. • Generally stays on target. • The whole prompt is in there somewhere.
Organization (Can your reader follow it?)	• Really high level words! • Tons of sentence types and lengths (texture). • Great transltlons (to quote, to commentary, between paragraphs). • Good use of paragraphs to divide ideas.	• Good, grade level vocabulary. • Some sentence variety. • A few transitions words or phrases here or there. • Uses multiple paragraphs.
Conventions (Do your errors get in the way?)	• Only a couple of errors (like a really good rough draft).	• Some errors, but they don't get in the way of what the reader understands.

Score 3 NOT QUITE, TRY HARDER	Score 2 ARE YOU LISTENING?	Score 1 EPIC FAIL
• Thesis is there, somewhere in the essay. • Only some evidence, but not for each point. • Only says in one line that there are those who disagree.	• What's this paper about? • No evidence (you didn't prove it!). • Not one mention of people who disagree with you.	
• Um, I think I get where you're going with this. • Drifts! • Tries to answer the prompt, but it's missing something.	• The reader doesn't follow you. • Blurry, like dirt on your glasses, unfocused. • Doesn't answer the prompt.	
• Simple vocab (good, happy, nice, fine, etc.). • Only one kind of sentence, and it gets boring in the rhythm. • Bumpy transitions! • Doesn't seem to understand why you need paragraphs.	• Repeats key words over and over. • Simple sentences. • No transitions (the reader must jump across gaps). • One LOOONNNGGGG paragraph.	Can't read it, not a persuasive essay.
• Lots of errors, but the reader can still understand what you mean.	• What the heck did the author mean by that?!	

Figure 7.5 is an example of a rubric that my elective, podcasting, uses. In this class, students create, write, perform, edit, produce, and publicize their own segments that make up a small group newscast. It can be rather amorphous; but as we know, in any tween classroom, seeming amorphousness is OK as long as there is embedded structure underneath the surface. Allowing them to have a hand in owning and designing the classroom rubric can help achieve this.

Figure 7.5. Student-Created Podcasting Rubric

Podcasting Rubric

If you receive any mark in the NR column, you will not make the deadline in this episode. Keep working and your show will be assessed again for a chance to air on Bulldog Radio.

Standard	Stupendous	Rockin'	Adequate	NR
L. Arts – 1.0 Word Fluency, Vocabulary Development *(We need to use high-level words in our writing)*				
L. Arts – 2.0 Reading Comprehension *(How well do I understand what I've read in my research?)*				
L. Arts – 3.0 Literary Response *(What is the quality of my book or movie review?)*				
L. Arts- 1.0 Listening and Speaking Strategies *(Do I sound professional? How is my speed and annunciation?)*				
L. Arts – 2.0 Oral Speaking Genres and Their Characteristics *(Does an ad sound like an ad and the news sound like the news? What is the mood or tone of my type of segment?)*				

Standard	Stupendous	Rockin'	Adequate	NR
Tech – 1 Basic Operations of Concepts *(Do you understand how to use Garageband and our other technology: iPods, headphones, etc?)*				
Tech – 2 Social, Ethical, and Human Issues *(Citing to avoid plagiarism, Internet safety strategies, and appropriate use of the computer)*				
Tech – 4 Technology Communication Tools *(How well do I use the microphone, the equalizer, etc. Am I aware of my voice in the colors?)*				
Tech – 5 Technology Research Tools *(How well do I use the computer to find out information? Am I able to figure out if the website is accurate?)*				
Tech – 6 Problem Solving and Decision Making *(Collaboration, working in small groups, student-led solutions: Did we solve our own problems?)*				
Specific Standard:				

In this case, I start with throwing up a "standards splat" on the board with all the possible English-Language Arts and Technology standards I can find. The kids chose the ones they thought were the most valuable and translated them. However, with podcasting, I found that I also needed to somehow differentiate the rubric, so I left a blank square at the bottom. This one is meant to be filled in by each student or partner pair based on the specific standard of their news show segment. For instance, if they were doing a book review, the standard would be different than that of a crossfire about a particular war. The students, therefore, research the appropriate standard and fill that in prior to their assessment.

Teach them how to translate rubrics into their own tween language. However, don't neglect the importance of hearing and understanding the academic adult language of the tests as well. To address this, have each of them also translate the rubrics created by other classes back into the language of their content area.

It's all about goal setting, being upfront with the students, and giving them ownership of their own learning by teaching them the secrets of teaching as a craft.

Student-Created Assessments

Has your well of quiz questions run dry? Are you struggling to breathe life into your assessments? Well, look no further. The answer lies in the talented pool of students who sit before you every day. Giving students tools to create the questions for some of your assessments empowers them in any number of ways:

1. It creates buy-in as they take the assessment themselves.

2. It teaches them the art of high-level questioning.

3. It allows them to see an assessment through a teacher's lens, thereby building up their ability to take future assessments beyond your classroom.

But if we're looking to build a rigorous, student-created assessment, it takes scaffolding mini-lessons on how to ask high-level questions. (See Chapter 10 for tips on how a student can develop higher levels of questions.)

Talking about levels of questioning also works toward another purpose: to demystify standardized testing. Inevitably, the students will discover that it's harder to create level 3 questions than level 1 questions. After all, recall is not as high as, say, apply or hypothesize, and what are most standardized tests? That's right. Recall, define, identify, etc.—that is, level 1. Many times it helps testing morale and is superempowering for students to learn that multiple-choice questions are potentially easier because the test makers are limited by their own format.

And speaking of format, this is a great time to teach the students about the formats of various assessments. For instance:

1. Rank Order Questions—"Please rank your knowledge of the following category from 1 to 5, 5 being best."

2. True/False

3. Fill-in-the-Blank

4. Matching

5. Short Answer

Explain that forced-choice questions actually give more power to the test maker. In other words, the students who are taking the test have no choice but to answer one way or another using only the choices provided by the test creator. Explain that open-ended questions like those that ask a student's opinion or those that ask "why" are more authentic but are harder to score. Explain, too, that if a test maker wants a test taker to stay focused during the assessment, the format of the questions ought to be varied; it keeps a test taker on their toes.

Once you've taught this concept of tiered leveled questions and have taught possible question formats, have the students create a list of questions to assess their knowledge of a concept. Use a revision-station-like rotation for peers to review the quality, word choice, grammatical accuracy, and spelling. Then have the student who authored the questions final draft them.

After the final drafts have been completed, have the students do one more activity: pass their questions to a peer and have the peer categorize the questions into level 1, 2, or 3 by marking in the margins. This will help students learn better recognition of higher-level questions and will help you when you select and assemble your final class assessment.

OK, so the kids have created the questions, revised or edited the questions, final drafted them, and categorized them. Now it's finally time to turn their lists of questions in to you. What you get is a stack of questions assessing your content created by the students themselves. But you still get the last word on the quality of the final test because you create the actual assessment by selecting from the students' questions. It's collaboration between teacher and student in its finest form.

By training students to work with your critical eye, they will, in turn, begin to produce work that is seen through your lens.

In fact, you can even create tests using questions from one period and give them out to another period rather than have the questions from a period be included in their own test. It's totally up to you, but it's created by them.

Figure 7.6 (page 96–101) is an example of a quiz created by my seventh graders for Gary Soto's "7th Grade."

So you've trained students to assess each other using the high standards of a critical thinker, and by training students to work with your critical eye, they will, in turn, begin to produce work that is seen through your lens.

Figure 7.6. Student-Created Test on Gary Soto's "7th Grade"

"7th Grade" Quiz by the 7th Grade

1. How would you compare Victor and Michael? _____
_____
_____

2. What do you think of Teresa as a character? Is she gullible or does she really know that Victor's bluffing? Use evidence to support your claim. ____
_____
_____
_____

3. List three adjectives that describe Victor: _____

☆☆☆☆☆

_____

4. Rate the story, 1 star being boring and 5 stars begin totally relatable.

5. OK, so let's pretend that you blurted out your crush's name in class while daydreaming. How would you feel? Use sensory details to describe what you would go through. _____
_____
_____
_____

6. List two pros and two cons about Victor and Teresa studying together:
   Pros _____
   Cons _____

7. What is the difference between a crush and love? _____
_____
_____

8. Circle the answer: How long would Victor and Teresa be together with this lie hanging between them?

   1 day   1 week   1 month   1 quarter   1 school year

9. Which character do you relate to more: Victor, Michael, Teresa, or Mr. Bueller? Why?_____

_____

_____

10. "Hi Victor," said Teresa.

"Yeah, that's me," replied Victor.

Write another response from Victor, one that he can feel better about.

_____

_____

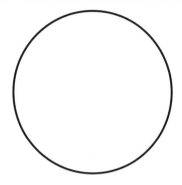

_____

11. Draw a person scowling.

Each of these activities and strategies is about preparing students for their future. They each focus on how to communicate, assess, collaborate, and create. In the end, as a culminating unit to assess each of these skills, I have devised a unit called "Teaching the Teacher," a multigenre project of sorts that assesses a student's ability to teach.

Teaching the Teacher Unit

It all begins with student choice. As we know, with tweens, adding their voice to the mix always means greater buy-in. They use what they've learned of persuasive writing to pitch a topic, any topic, as something they want to teach me and their fellow students. By asking them to write a persuasive essay including thesis statement, reasons, and counterargument, you tend to weed out some more silly suggestions.

Some of the best topics that students have wanted to teach are the following:

1. How to Solve a Rubik's Cube

2. The History of the Lakers

3. How to Make Enchiladas

4. How to Play Guitar Hero

5. The History of Skateboarding

I call it a multigenre unit because the end result actually requires a student to produce different genres of assessment. By the end of the unit, the student will have done the following:

1. **Develop a Lesson Plan.** This lesson plan consists of that which you would expect as a teacher. Sure, it can be tedious for us to produce lesson plans for each lesson we present, but by breaking it down into its parts, you can see how valuable it would be to a student just learning how to describe, sequence, summarize, etc. It includes:

   - A stated *objective*

   - A list of *materials*

   - A summarized *lesson description*

   - A *step-by-step description* of the lesson

2. **Present an Oral Presentation of Their Lesson to the Class.** This oral presentation must be a combination of different examples of multiple intelligences. It must include a visual of some kind (PowerPoint, poster, video, etc.). It must include an activity for the students in the classroom (or representatives pulled from the captive audience of peers.) For instance, perhaps the class lines up at a free throw line, and after observing the student model how to throw a great free throw, they are given the opportunity, one by one, to try their hand at the task.

3. **Create and Administer a Ten-Question Quiz to Us All.** After presenting their lesson, the student must administer a quiz to the class that shows examples of different levels of questions as well as questions that are varied in format. The student must then, as a homework assignment, go home and score the quizzes from the class. This does not count as a quiz for each student, but rather as a participation or classwork grade. After all, it is meant to assess the student as a teacher and to keep the class accountable for behavior and focus during the lesson's presentation.

4. **Write a Persuasive Business Letter to an Administrator.** This final component of the Teaching the Teacher unit is an authentic assessment wherein the student writes a letter to an administrator to convince him or her that their activity or hobby or what-

ever should be an elective at the school. In the past, I have gotten administrators to agree to score ten papers each based on our Persuasive Essay rubric. It was great to assign students, with great drama, to pitch to different people on the school site or at the district level: the principal, the two assistant principals, a board member, or even the superintendent. Sure, it was a mythical program, but many of the administrators actually got into it, highlighting their feedback on the rubric prior to issuing a score, and even writing comments as to why or why not they would consider the addition of such an elective. Here is a comment written by our principal in response to one such persuasive letter:

> No, sorry Brian. We won't be offering naptime as an elective for next year. I do, however, appreciate your research on the sleep needs of the average middle schooler, and I was also very interested in your studies of dream symbolism. Nevertheless, naptime, however necessary, is, unfortunately, not covered in the state standards, and will not be on the master calendar for next year.

Having the students write to other members of the educational community creates not only authenticity, but also a community that extends beyond your classroom. It also lets folks know of the great stuff going on in your own classroom. I highly recommend involving as many people as possible in this final step as a means to publicize yourself and your class's accomplishments. (See Chapter 14 for more on publicizing your efforts.)

In the end, the Teaching the Teacher unit is meant to assess students not only on content but also on communication, and it's this very act of being able to communicate content that we should all be striving to assess. After all, when these students leave our year behind, eventually leaving school behind entirely, they must take with them the ability to share, to create, to assess, to problem solve, to research…to teach.

Ours is the profession that teaches all others. Prepare them with this in mind, and you will have had a hand in whatever their future holds.

8

Tips for Developing a Tween-Centric Classroom Library for Any Subject

A room without books is like a body without a soul.
— Marcus Tullius Cicero

I believe that a classroom library is the heartbeat of every teacher's environment. It is the window into their own personality and reflects the importance of literacy in the classroom. Furthermore, I believe every teacher—math, history, robotics, French, or any other subject—should have a grade A, top-notch classroom library.

For one thing, having a great library promotes student achievement (our #1 goal), and for another, it introduces the students to what you love. That knowledge of you and that possible connection to them makes teaching easier; and easier teaching can contribute to your level of happiness in this otherwise difficult job (goal #2).

It's pretty obvious why building a classroom library builds student achievement. After all, it promotes literacy, and the more classrooms that support that goal, the better. According to Donalyn Miller, author of *The Book Whisperer* (Jossey-Bass, 2009), "Access to books is a key factor in promoting reading and motivating children to read." Additionally, having a classroom library also promotes differentiation, giving those children readily accessible choice in their independent reading.

Although I'm partly talking about introducing tweens to a wide range of books, I'm also talking about introducing tweens to a wide range of teachers. After all, each classroom library has the personality of its owner. The more libraries to choose from, the more chances a student has to connect with both their literature and their teachers.

To build a classroom library can be a long process, and one that can be as addictive as any drug. As soon as you commit to its importance, it becomes an obsession, a collection to which you are forever adding. It's all worth it to introduce a new batch into the classroom, reading the blurbs and summaries with great suspense, showing the class the cover art just to see the eagerness of the faces and the trembling hands quickly raised just for the honor of being the first student to check out a new book you've entered into the library. To help you begin and maintain this process, this chapter discusses these topics:

- ◆ The four categories of readers
- ◆ Starting and financing your classroom library
- ◆ Attracting tweens to your classroom library
- ◆ Checking Out Books
- ◆ Generating interest in your classroom library
- ◆ Helping a student choose a book

Developing a classroom library that reflects your interests is clearly a draw to inherent readers. Additionally, you might find that you also share interests with harder-to-reach students, which is something you can tap into. Shared interest with a teacher creates students who are more eager to be in your space; and if they are eager to be there, they are easier to teach in a deeper way.

The Four Categories of Readers

I believe that there are ranges of student readers, and access to books should be thought about with the same differentiated approach as any other lesson, assessment, or activity. Along those lines, I've identified what appears to me to be four categories of readers who all relate to books in different ways:

1. **The Brash Bibliophile**—These are students who are well versed in the language of book choice and seek out what they want, avidly asking questions or using learned or inherent strategies to find the book that will make them hide under their sheets at night with a flashlight in hand. They will find their way to their local bookstore by any means necessary, and look through the stacks until their parents pull them away. They know how to choose books, to set their own level, and aren't intimidated by books that are above their reading level. Picking a book that proves too difficult will not deter them from picking up another book.

2. **The Public Library Literate**—These are students who won't or can't go to a store, but who will go to the local library. They, too,

have a facility with literacy and are comfortable with seeking out a book, or perhaps asking a question or two from a familiar face. Perhaps they have spent summers or after-school hours in a library. Perhaps they've volunteered in a library. Perhaps they take their younger sibling to the library. For whatever reason, they have an ease walking around the stacks and checking out books. They find the aisles they like, the shelves they like, and exhaust them. If they run out, they've been to the library so often that they feel somewhat comfortable asking a librarian or aide for help finding another genre or book.

3. **The Lunchtime Lurker**—These are students who may only be comfortable at the school library. Perhaps their comfort began while avoiding the social obstacles of school lunches. However, what began as a safe zone out of developmental fear, developed into an appreciation of the dark corners of the school stacks, discovering this character or that plot line, waiting to swipe their ID card and get the book back home at the bell.

4. **The Fretful Phobic**—Then there are students who are so frightened of books, of literacy, and of choice, that they only barely feel comfortable in their own classroom library. They know they can ask their teacher because their teacher knows them, relates to them, and can advise them. They begin by reaching for books that don't challenge them but are fun. Maybe they read and re-read and reread the *Diary of a Wimpy Kid* books (who can blame them?) and they know exactly where to find what they love. They learn to trust in your advice and confidential knowledge of their fears and literacy insecurities. They continue to grab the same books for lack of any other book they can confidently enjoy. We need to start from scratch with these kids and teach them how to choose a book (see below).

It's up to us, the classroom teachers, to attract all these students like moths to a flame. However, even the best teacher can't possibly connect with every student. Nevertheless, odds are that every student can find at least one teacher each year that they do like and relate to. Just imagine the power on any school site if all teachers had classroom libraries that reflected them, so that every young reader could find somewhere comfortable to get access to the literacy that he or she needs.

Starting and Financing Your Classroom Library

It might seem hard to start a library from scratch. Nevertheless, try to remember that unless we do, the voracious appetites of tween readers may also be affected by this economic downturn. After all, with budget cuts tightening everybody's belt, many parents can't go to bookstores. Public libraries are slowly closing, snuffed out one-by-one by lack of funding and support. Scholastic Book Fairs have become mere mirages on the horizon that, when the date approaches, disappears with waves rising off of the pavement with apologies of "no money." However, our job of turning kids onto readers still continues. Teachers, proverbial swords in hand, must carry the standard of literacy despite our own empty pockets.

But don't despair! You need not choose your classroom library over your cell phone bill. Although it continuously stuns me that more funds aren't provided by schools and districts for teachers of every discipline to develop their own stacks, there are ways to jumpstart your collection.

> *You need not choose your classroom library over your cell phone bill.*

For instance, earlier in my career, as soon as I realized how important it was to build my own classroom library, I first turned to my own childhood books that I had kept in boxes at my parents' house to begin filling my first bookshelf.

You remember those boxes, right? For me, I was reminded of them about five years after I moved out of my parents' house, getting a call from my dad that went as follows, "It's time. Come get the boxes under the house. They're driving us crazy." And even though my parents never ventured forth under the house, and even though I only lived in a one-bedroom apartment with a futon and a desk at the time, I packed up the boxes and gave them a new home: my newborn classroom library.

Sure they were dusty. Sure some had water damage. But they had pages, and they reflected the books I had been able to read when I had been a tween, and I had read them all, which meant I could talk about them with the knowledge of characters and plots. I even shared what I recalled about the time in my life in which I read them or a memory that their reading conjured up.

I slowly added to my ancient collection by going to every book bargain basement sale I stumbled on. You'd be surprised how many are around. I also developed a very charming book-begging letter, seeking out books from friends and family (see Figure 8.2, page 105). I never asked for money, but I did ask for books. Word of warning, when you ask friends and family if they have books, you're bound to get more than you could ever pick up in your car.

Start by building your classroom library a little at a time. To get you going, I've created a little seven-step cheat sheet for quick reminders of what to do to start that library off right.

1. Start with bringing in what books you still have (make sure if they are precious that you put a "Do Not Check Out" sticker on their spines).

2. Tour local flea markets (I've even found first edition classics at flea markets, so be on the lookout for great reads and great illustrations).

3. Go to bargain basement sales at your local bookstore.

4. Check out your local library sales—$1 books are frequent, so go back often.

5. Use the school book fair, if it's available. If you are asked to make a wish list, do it. Even if only one parent fulfills a book on the list, it still generates interest in your library.

6. Definitely take advantage of the Scholastic Book 4000-point trick—OK, here's a little publicized tid-bit of awesomeness: Occasionally, Scholastic Book Clubs offers twenty times the bonus points for every $200 earned. That means that if you can raise $200 using just one catalogue (or combined with the efforts of another teacher using the same catalogue) you will get 4000 bonus points to inject free books into your classroom library. Figure 8.1 is my letter home explaining my goals at the beginning of the year for this little-known book-buying nugget of knowledge.

Figure 8.1. My Scholastic Book Club Letter

Dear Students and Families,

We all know that reading is important. It expands our world and helps to improve our writing. But many students do not have access to literature at home, or cannot afford to buy books themselves. For this reason, I believe it is my responsibility to provide an exciting reading environment and many reading opportunities for my students. I have done this by developing the most AWESOME classroom library on campus.

It includes books that I have purchased myself, books from my own childhood, and books from my son's own home library. It is a great collection of literature, but to continue to attract students throughout the year, it must continue to grow.

Whenever a new book comes in, it is always checked out immediately, sucked up by some reader like a vacuum. I want to give more students that opportunity.

Which brings me to you. This month, Scholastic Book Club is offering 4000 free bonus points to any classroom teacher who orders $200 worth of books. I have approximately 250 students this year. So if I do the math correctly, I only need ¼ to ½ of my students to order 1 book each in order to reach that goal.

The prize will end up being 100 to 200 free books for my classroom library. My students will help in selecting and recommending the books, and in so doing, they will be a part of the reading memories that future students will have for years to come.

Please consider ordering from Scholastic this month. The deadline is September 26. You can write a check to Scholastic Book Clubs or you can give me cash to place the order. Either way, you will be helping your own student by giving them a book that they can excitingly look forward to getting, and you will be helping out the classroom library as well.

Thank you for participating in this program, and for helping give the gift of literacy.

Sincerely,

Heather Wolpert-Gawron

7th & 8th Grade ELA teacher

Speech & Debate/Podcasting Coach

7. Beg—Beg books from family and from friends. People are always looking to get rid of books and nobody wants to throw them out. Offer to take them off of their hands and it's a win–win. Figure 8.2 is a copy of my book-begging letter, which I have sent out to family and friends in the past. Fortunately, our local library has since reopened with great activity from the community, but the more detail you put in your letter, the better. Feel free to use it to build your own classroom library.

Figure 8.2. My Book-Begging Letter

Hello family and friends,

As many of you know, I am a middle school teacher in San Gabriel. We are a Title I district. What this means is that there is a large percentage of our students who are on a federally provided meal plan based on their low-income status. We cater to an amazing array of learners, from GATE to at-risk students, serving a wide demographic, a large portion of which are English language Learners. They all want to learn, and it is my job to teach them.

But, unbelievably, San Gabriel has no bookstores. The nearest Barnes and Noble is in Temple City and the nearest Borders is in Arcadia. (Both districts are, not coincidentally, scoring higher in their standardized tests. Some might find this a weak link. I, however, believe there to be an undeniable correlation.) San Gabriel's public library has been closed for a year for renovations.

I believe that part of my responsibility as an English teacher is to enable opportunities for students to discover books they love. One of the best ways to do this is to surround them with literature and drown them in a book-rich environment.

I have spent my last ten years as a teacher building my own classroom library theme park. I have spent many an hour at bookstores, bargain tables, and flea markets looking to inject my classroom library with titles to interest students of all levels and interests. For without new books to explore, the excitement for a library dies.

I am writing today to ask for books. I am looking for nicely used books in your own libraries or children's libraries that everyone has outgrown or has lost interest in. I am looking for books in every genre, in every level. I have students, after all, who are reading at the fourth grade level and those who are reading at the twelfth grade level. I want to challenge them all.

If you have ANYTHING, please let me know and I'll come by, look through your collection, and take as many of them off your hands as I can use. No number is too small to call. Even if I can only capture a couple of books from this plea, a few new books will go a long way toward exciting a class to reexplore an entire classroom library.

Thank you for considering donating books to my classroom library. I promise you that many students will read them for many years to come. One day, the books may fall apart with use, but there is no better death for a book then having been read too much by too many.

Much love,
Heather

Attracting Tweens to Your Classroom Library

The first thing that attracts a student to the library is its appearance, but the thing that keeps them coming back for more are the books.

The minute a student walks through your door and looks around, it's all about "presentation, presentation, presentation." In my library, all the shelves are peppered with realia from my own life. Realia refers to artifacts, those tangible objects that educators or those in the library sciences may use to illustrate a point or topic. The realia on my shelves highlights the genres in my library. On my shelves, for instance, lie the dolls and action figures of my youth, as well as the little knickknacks and trinkets I've picked up along the way. There's even the occasional gift from a student who, while on vacation, actually thought about my classroom library while passing by a kiosk in England or a gift shop in China.

Perched at the end of my mystery section sits a silly Snoopy Sherlock Holmes Hallmark doll some student gave me. The touristy Artemis statuette I got in eighth grade when my family went to Greece sits next to my mythology section. The Shakespeare action figure with removable quill action sits between a full-text edition of *Midsummer Night's Dream* and the Manga version of *As You Like It*. My Jane Austin action figure reclines amongst my historical fiction. My sixth grade Clash of the Titans lunch box bookends fantasy. A figurehead of Captain Morgan that hung in my room all through high school glares down at "any who dare not use the proper means of checking out a book." The statue of "The Raven" that a student gave me (which, I never told her, was really a pigeon) sits next to my Poe action figure. I have an old Viewmaster with slides of the National Parks to inspire Quickwrites and a deck of cards called "Old English Insults." They're all there. Each little tchotchke has a purpose. Each helps to entrap my students into the web of literacy that is my classroom library.

Make sure there are some books facing forward, displaying their cover art. I know this sounds like something from an elementary school classroom, but it's all about the pitch, and some methods that work in elementary can also work with middle school. Make the library sexy and it will draw those kids in without you having to say a word. Line the whole top of the shelves with forward-facing books, and even the occasional edition embedded between tomes, to pitch books to those students who aren't attracted by rows and rows of book spines. Take a tip from bookstores and create displays.

In regard to choices, my stacks have every genre at every level, clearly marked with stickers to represent each category. That way, there is a language to finding and filing the books with ease, even for the most struggling of readers.

In my library, every genre makes an appearance, sending the message that every genre counts: books, comic books, graphic novels, magazine articles, picture books, etc. After all, when I was in middle school I went through different stages. I read *Around the World in 80 Days* for school, but I was reading *Elf Quest*, the graphic novel, at home. I also was reading *Animal Farm* and *Seventeen*. Reading begets reading.

In the end, you'll create a corner of your room that teaches literacy through sheer osmosis.

In the end, you'll create a corner of your room that teaches literacy through sheer osmosis. The environment of the classroom is vital in its success. It is Think Aloud without speaking. It tells the students who you are and what you're about as a teacher. It says, "books are important here, and literacy is a priority."

Checking Out Books

OK, they're hooked. They find a book that they *must* read now. But how do you keep the books safe and still give students access? Well, there are many ways to control the ebb and flow of books into and out of your classroom library. Here are some of the systems I've used or have seen used. They all have pros and cons. Pick the one that works best for you.

1. **Index Cards**—A student fills out an index card with Title, Name, and Date and drops it into a file labeled with their period number. When the book is returned, the student shows me they are filing the book on the correct genre shelf and are then, with permission, allowed to tear up their slip. I do a monthly read-off of names to see if books are being read or when they will be returned.

Figure 8.3 is a copy of my checkout slip. Feel free to copy it to your heart's content.

Figure 8.3. My Simple Book Checkout Form

Book Checkout
Student Name: _____
Period: _____
Title to Be Checked Out: _____
Today's Date: _____

2. **LendMe**—This iPhone app (Figure 8.4) is great for smaller class sizes, as I have found that even the most reluctant readers are excited to use it. When I taught summer school, for instance, it was easy to use it with my smaller numbers of students. The way it works is this: The student takes a book from the shelf, I click on the app, take a picture of the kid and the book, type in the date, and it's recorded until the book is returned and I delete the entry. I say do this only with smaller classes because the ideal situation has kids in charge of their own checkout without bothering you in order to do so. Using LendMe definitely has you doing the work.

Figure 8.4. LendMe iPhone App

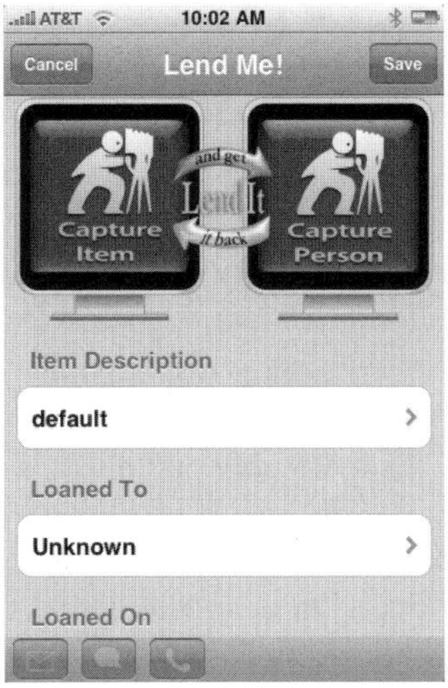

3. **Seating Chart with Sticky Notes**—I always liked the following method, even if it relied a little heavily on the teacher: Keep a binder with the seating charts for each of your classes in it. Keep a stack of little sticky notes handy and each time a kid checks out a book, write their name and the title and stick it on their "desk" in your binder. When the student returns the book, simply pick up the sticky note and toss it. What I like about this is that it's so visual. But the drawback is that it has the teacher doing the checking in and out, and my goal is to teach the students responsibility without increasing my own workload.

Begin experimenting with the checkout process that works for you and that doesn't take a lot of time and energy in the middle of your day. Ask your students for suggestions. In fact, you can make it a mini-lesson about genre, about what they've last read, about persuasive writing, anything that helps them to own and run the library too.

Generating Interest in Your Classroom Library

Having the library isn't enough, however; you also have to shake it up a bit every once in a while. After all, the students will go through surges of interest, then that excitement will die down. Therefore, it's up to you to bring the library back to life and back to their attention. Now, a new influx of books will always create renewed excitement about the classroom library, but you can't keep feeding the beast just to generate hunger.

Here are some activities to encourage reading and promote renewed interest, that won't come out of your pocket, are standards-based, and student-driven:

1. **Reading Genre Posters**—Taking a tip from iPod ads (black silhouettes on bright, solid-colored backgrounds), I've got my seventh graders reviewing the reading genres by creating Reading Genre Posters. We begin by brainstorming genres and their characteristics. Then small groups pick which ones they want to produce. We discuss ways in which groups can reach consensus (see Chapter 2), and the kids each have to design a poster possibility, select it as a group, and execute it. Some students cut, some are the models lying down on the paper, posed like a superhero (comics) or a mermaid (fantasy) or swinging on a vine (adventure). Some draw, and some record how the group functions. At the end, we review the reading genres and have these projects up in time for Back-to-School night.

2. **Book Spines**—To prove the frequency of their reading, have the students continuously, throughout the year, fill out "book spines" to visually display their efforts. Just provide them with the book spine template, then they fill out the TAG (Title, Author, Genre) and perhaps decorate the spine with symbols representing the book. Then they staple the book spine on the wall in a line, leaned against each other, stacked, etc., just like a shelf of books. If you want, each book spine can be a raffle entry and you can pull names out of a hat or do something else at the end of the quarter for a reading reward. Your call. By the end of the year, they will have created their own bookshelves, overwhelming the classroom with proof of their literacy.

3. **Celebrate Banned Books Week**—This one can be tricky depending upon where you teach and the opinions of your local community, so make sure you have an understanding about your neighbors before moving forward on this activity. Go to the American Library Association website (www.ala.org/books) and read the list of books that have been censored or about which a complaint has been filed. Slap a huge red label that says, "Banned!" on any book in your classroom library that appears on the list. The bigger deal you make of what books in your classroom library have appeared on a banned books list at some point, the more kids you will have scrambling to read them.

4. **Scavenger Hunts**—When interest tapers off, I start my classroom library scavenger hunts with questions on the board like these:

1. Find the book with the Map of Gilder inside its front cover. (Answer: *The Princess Bride*)

2. Which author appears on the most genre shelves? (Answer: *Avi*)

3. Which book on Mrs. Wolpert's fantasy shelf inspired the book, *Wendy*? Follow up to question #3: What is the title of the biography about that fantasy book's author? (Answer: *J.M. Barrie and the Lost Boys*)

5. **Involve Your Library**—Include your library in your lessons. Have the students pull their favorite lines from the books for homework assignments. Have the kids find hooks from books in the library, write them on index cards, and then randomly select one to use as a starting line for their next narrative.

6. **Advertise Your Library**—Have the students design persuasive ads to get other students to read a book that they may have loved.

Notice I never mentioned the traditional reading log. I'm just not a fan. If it works for you, great. I'm just not interested in demanding something I can't enforce. I just think it shackles kids to monotone quantity production instead of encouraging them to communicate comprehension. I think many teachers do reading logs to appease parents. I think it's one of those vestiges from a bygone educational era that so many of us were brought up with, and it's one of those long-term assignments that parents relate to because they had to do it, too. It's a common language between parents and teachers, and because it's recognizable, it's not controversial. However, I'm not sold on how it relates to student achievement. Nonetheless, if it works for you, and you've found a way reading logs really help students read better, *kina hora* (more power to you) as my grandmother used to say.

Here's what I do instead, and rather than give them a reading score based on one log, I fold in other assignments as assessments of their reading (mind you, it's still a work in progress, but I find it at least works better for me then the log):

♦ **The Bibliography Book**—Students add a correct bibliographical entry to the back of their Writers Notebook when they finish reading a book, magazine, comic, graphic novel, or website. They are assessed on their ability to write a proper bibliography as well as their growing list of books.

♦ **Golden Line Assignments**—These are periodic assignments due at the beginning of the period that assess their ability to recognize certain skills we're studying in their independent reading books. For instance, when we studied sensory details, the students needed to hunt for an example from their independent reading books and write it on an index card. They line up at the door (so nobody could invisibly scramble to fill theirs in while I am collecting the cards) and as they enter, they fold and drop their cards into a "Golden Line Jar." Then, with great flourish, I pull one out and use it to promote discussion about that sentence or skill.

+ **One-Pagers**—These are assessments done in one to two periods that show what a student knows about his or her book, all on one 8.5×11 page. On that one page, they have to create a symbolic image, pull two quotes, write commentary on those quotes, and develop a question related to the book. It's unintimidating, it's quick, and it's both a linguistic and nonlinguistic assessment of reading comprehension.

There are tons of differentiated alternatives out there for logs and books reports. So go forth and demand more than just what the reading log gives you.

In addition to reading logs, there's also something else I don't do. I don't organize my library by levels. Leveling a library drives me a little nuts. Some of the best teachers I know have done it; but, again, this is just what works for me. Personally, I would rather teach students how to choose books that are both accessible yet slightly challenging. Then you have given them the ownership to define their own level.

Helping a Student Choose a Book

Any tween classroom has a ginormous range of ability levels and interests. Yet we must cater to them all. Each student needs to know that somewhere in your stacks, amongst the props, the displays, the stickers, and the ads, sits their next book, ready to be discovered. As Donalyn Miller shared with me, "Students at all levels must be able to find a wide range of material that they are capable of reading. Books should explore a range of topics and genres so that children can locate books that engage their attention...." But no kid can just pick up any book and love it. That's where you come in. Beyond your own recommendations, you also must teach a student how to choose a book that's right for him or her.

Generally I start by putting a pile of books on each table group. Before rotating the books or the students, I have them do the following:

1. Check out the cover art—Is it a photo? A drawing? Does it use symbolism? Is it interesting?

2. Read the blurb at the back of the book—Does it tell you the whole story? Does it keep you wanting more? Does it end in a statement or a question? Is it followed by quotes or reviews?

3. Skim the table of contents—Are the chapter titles interesting?

4. Skim the first few pages—Are you already hooked?

5. Follow the Five-Finger Rule—To determine if a book is too easy or too hard, have the student flip to a random page in the book. If there are at least five words on the page that the student doesn't know, it's probably above their head and may prove frustrating. If there are no challenging words, well, then, it may be too easy for that student. However, that's not to say that a too easy book (*Diary of a Wimpy Kid*) or a too difficult book (*The Lord of the Flies*) might not be loved by the student; it's all about the student going in to a new reading adventure with as much knowledge as he or she can so the student doesn't get set up for disappointment.

Surround them in literacy, acknowledge their own passions, and they may be more likely to explore the library beyond the boundaries of their own interests. I think that so much about encouraging literacy is about making it enticing. Make reading attractive and make it unavoidable to enjoy. Make it so that every classroom they walk into has one, and in the end, you'll be working as a staff to improve student achievement together. By offering up a little of your own personality to the altar of student knowledge, you will make your classroom a more comfortable place to be for you and your students.

The classroom library should be an interactive part of your classroom. One day the books may fall apart with use, but remember what I said in my book-begging letter: there is no better death for a book than having been read too much by too many.

9

Tips for Differentiation in a Tween Classroom

America has believed that in differentiation, not in uniformity, lies the path of progress. It acted on this belief; it has advanced human happiness, and it has prospered.

— Louis D. Brandeis

I used to be scared of differentiation. That is, until I started doing it. Before, I used to imagine some classroom filled with inboxes reflecting every possible option for each lesson, a tracked version of segregation that added ten times the work to my workload and prep time for each and every lesson. I imagined it to be something like this:

> If you are interested in cars, your activity can be found in the blue box. If you are drawn more to the culinary arts, please look in the yellow inbox. If you like to doodle in the margins, please find your next activity in the red box, and if you are still scoring below basic on your reading assessment, you can find your activity in the green box.

But now I know that differentiation isn't like that. I now see it as increasing buy-in, easing struggles in my classroom management because the students are interested, and bumping up achievement because the cards are stacked in their favor. I also see differentiation as introducing students to modalities and styles that are *not* their choice, preparing students for a world of many different people and many different variable paths. I also see it as a way to challenge students to look beyond themselves, learn about others, and in so doing, learn to feel less intimidated functioning outside of their comfort zone.

But do we really have to create thirty-six different lessons for thirty-six different kids 180 days a year? Of course not. What we do have to do is vary our presentation and our expectations, mix it up a bit from our own tendencies, if we are to reach out to the diverse learners in our tween classrooms.

And diverse it is. After all, the snapshot of a tween classroom is the picture of a student smorgasbord. So how does one differentiate in a classroom that is home to both a fifth grade-level reader and a twelfth grade-level reader? Well, for one thing, allowing students choice is a huge part of differentiation and it allows you to tailor a lesson to each student by inviting them into the lesson design itself. However, to invite them into designing their own differentiation takes teaching students first about who they are as learners. Therefore, in this chapter, we explore these topics:

♦ Understanding the learners in the classroom (including yourself)

♦ Designing differentiated lessons

Some would say using differentiation is a more difficult way to teach, but I say that it's the more interesting way to teach, not just for the students, but also for us; and what's more engaging and enjoyable for us is bound to be a more effective way to reach the most students.

Understanding the Learners in the Classroom (Including Yourself)

Differentiating in the classroom takes three important steps:

1. Realizing, as a teacher, your own tendencies as a learner;

2. Discovering how your students learn; and

3. Allowing students to utilize their own learning methods.

I believe that true differentiation begins with your own analysis of who you, the teacher, are as a learner. To design lessons that reflect and engage all of your students, you need to reflect on who you were as a learner and what style of teaching towards which you easily gravitate. What worked for you as a student might not be what works for all of your students. Be open to learning more about who you are and how you naturally learn, and in so doing, you can purposefully and proactively target lesson delivery that attracts a different kind of learner than you.

> *I believe that true differentiation begins with your own analysis of who you, the teacher, are as a learner.*

It's important at this point, before we talk about lesson design, to clarify a key difference between these two phrases that seem to be used interchangeably, but yet in all actuality, refer to different concepts: learning styles vs. multiple intelligences. Thus, before we go on, I want to provide a quickie definition of the two so that we can use them properly in our mental common language dictionary.

The bottom line difference between them is this: Learning styles refers to how you might learn best whereas multiple intelligences is more about how you might demonstrate that learning best (see Figure 9.1).

Figure 9.1. Learning Styles vs. Multiple Intelligences

Learning Styles	Multiple Intelligences
Visual	*Linguistic*—using language (words, writing)
	Logical—using science and math (numbers)
	Musical—using tone and rhythm
	Bodily-Kinesthetic—using sports and movement
Auditory	*Visual-Spatial*—using art, design, and shapes
	Interpersonal—using the ability to communicate well with other people
Tactile/Kinesthetic	*Intrapersonal*—using a deep understanding of yourself, being reflective
	Naturalist—using your knowledge and appreciation of nature and the world beyond you

OK, now that we know the difference between the two concepts, I want you to put them aside. I'm not saying that these topics aren't important, but I am saying that you shouldn't get too caught up in the details of nomenclature. Students shouldn't be academically segregated by a Learning Styles or Multiple Intelligences definition. In fact, I think it's far more important that students learn lots of different ways to learn, and the only way for them to do that is for you to teach in many different ways. It makes them more flexible as learners and it keeps things spontaneous in the classroom. This adds to overall engagement and that translates to achievement.

After all, none of us are ever an all-or-nothing deal. It's not like you are 0% linguistic and 100% visual-spatial. That's an important distinction, because it means that students as learners, and you as a teacher, can grow and develop in the categories that might not come naturally to either of you.

Frankly, I think that there's a danger in allowing ourselves to settle into our innate intelligences. It's like going to the gym, building up your left bicep, but leaving the rest of your body as flab. If you don't exercise it all, you'll never find out what the rest of your body can do. Just as you need to work on every body muscle, so should you work out your whole brain. Just as you can easily develop some lessons in one modality, so should you develop lessons that represent other modalities.

OK, so you've reflected about who you were as a learner and what your tendencies as a teacher are so that you can push yourself to diversify your lessons. The next step is to discover how your students learn. To do so takes more than just looking at their cumulative folders and test scores. It's about watching them interact as young adults with emerging opinions and thoughts. Sure you can research their previous test scores, but to really aid you in your lesson design, you have to look beyond the scores and into the hearts of the students themselves. This takes researching them in other ways, a character scavenger hunt of sorts.

I find that the best time to really get to know my tweens is before school. They may not be totally awake yet, but you can use that to your advantage. When they're tired, they haven't yet built up their social caffeine. Maybe their friends have yet to arrive. Who else is there to talk to besides you? Maybe you aren't their first choice of someone to hang out with, but on a chilly morning, heater on in the classroom, you'd be amazed at how many kids want to come in and hang out for fifteen minutes, and you can learn a lot about those kids in that amount of time.

In the morning, the rule is clear, if you're in my room before the first bell, you're fair game to be put to work; and it's no surprise that while we're shelving books or cutting paper and helping me prep for my Language Arts classes, I learn *a lot*.

I learn who is dating whom; what fights are scheduled; how they feel about other kids and classes; who has Saturday school; and about schools kids might be transferring to before it happens. It's amazing how lucid and chatty a middle schooler can be in the thirty minutes before school. It's like the calm before the storm.

I learn how they've spent their weekend. Maybe they went to a museum or camping. Maybe they helped to build a deck. Or maybe they simply played 72 hours of video games and want to talk about their virtual victories. Who knows, but it's my opportunity to learn about the education that my students receive while living outside of school.

> *It's amazing how lucid and chatty a middle schooler can be in the thirty minutes before school. It's like the calm before the storm.*

Now, once you've started learning things about those tweens who sit before you every day, keep a simple binder or yellow pad of notes about what you learn. It doesn't have to be some big, formal list with standardized columns of information for each kid. Nope. I'm talking about some simple observations about how the kids learn. It's only for your benefit, so there's no deadline or due date. My yellow pad looks something like this:

♦ Neil learns better if I'm teaching with the Interactive Board and totally phases out when we're reading.

- Desiree phases out when we're reading, but as long as someone's talking about the material, she's in.

- Tien thrives in the computer lab.

- The entire class wakes up if they stand up.

- Seth is like a bike; he has to be going fast and doing three things at once or he can't pay attention at all and falls over, bored.

- Armando needs everything to relate to him or he goes over to the Dark Side.

- Jenny will do anything academic I ask of her as long as I allow her to use a pink pen.

- Brandon will never be given the time of day, and nobody will love his writing like I do, unless he learns to type.

- Every student loves coming in to find the room looking different.

- Sarah will work with Angy. Angy will work with Fabiola and Sarah. But Fabiola can't work with Sarah.

- Tin will function in a small group, but only one consisting of young ladies.

OK, so this isn't the most scientifically based study in the world, but it's the one that works in my classroom. It's the different learners in my class, as analyzed by me.

These observations can take place informally, but you can also strategically design a lesson that hits different modalities and analyze the results of the project to learn a lot about the tendencies of your students. One of the really quick differentiated get-to-know lessons I do early in the year begins in the first day or two of school.

After all, going over class rules does not teach me who they are. Going over routines and rituals does not tell me who they are. However, having them immediately do an activity that forces them to follow step-by-step directions, eyes on me, and that at the end requires them to answer questions about themselves, does give me vital information about them from minute one. Consequently, one of the earliest activities I assign is one that builds on the multiple intelligences right away: the booker.

The booker is a foldable that ends up looking like a book, but starts out a simple sheet of paper. Figure 9.2 shows how to create a booker.

Figure 9.2. The Booker

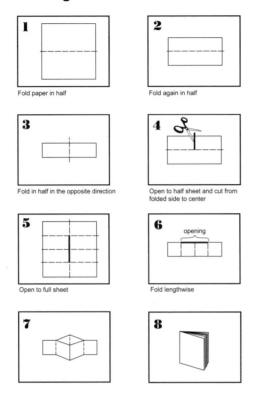

Once completed, mark the pages as follows:

1. **Cover:** Create an illuminated letter (show them pictures of illuminated letters as you talk). The letter should be a block letter, the first one in the first name. The symbols should represent their interests.

2. **Pages 1 and 2:** Create a timeline of the major events in your life.

3. **Page 3:** Write three adjectives that describe you.

4. **Page 4:** Create a haiku about yourself.

5. **Page 5:** Write three sentences about a flaw in your character that you admit you have.

6. **Page 6:** Create an alliteration out of your first or last name.

7. **Page 7:** Write a paragraph about a time of which you are the most proud.

When the bookers are done, you can collect them and analyze which students excelled at which little directives. You'll find some students write a beautiful haiku, but their illuminated letter is really sloppy. You'll find some students are already reflective and can recognize their own flaws, whereas others create a very detailed timeline. It all equates to an informal assessment for you of who they are as learners.

Now take it one step further and help students increase their own knowledge of differentiation. After all, if their awareness of the strategies goes up, then those strategies will be embedded even further.

I like students to take surveys about their likes and dislikes. It gives them a little data about themselves to work with. There are tons of interactive quizzes out there, quizzes and surveys that have them answering questions about themselves, and as you know, the topic that middle schoolers are most interested in is themselves.

According to some surveys, four colors have been used to define the differences between personalities: gold, blue, green, and orange. Eight slices of a pie have been used to categorize the different intelligences: linguistic, logical, naturalistic, interpersonal, intrapersonal, visual/spatial, kinesthetic, musical. Three descriptions have been used to define learning styles: auditory, visual, and tactile.

It's frankly fascinating for students to discover they are "green," "interpersonal," and "auditory." It makes them feel unique yet understood. Give them the outlet and they will be engaged.

Here are two interactive quiz resources, if you're so inclined:

♦ http://www.edutopia.org/multiple-intelligences-learning-styles-quiz

♦ http://www.truecolorscareer.com/quiz.asp

Beyond interactive quizzes, I've also started experimenting with having the students create their own multi-intelligence quizzes by developing new categories as a means to learn about who they are. I admit it; I was inspired by Facebook.

On Facebook, a person can be infinitely defined by any thematic quiz imaginable. The way I see it, however, it's just the same old—same old personality-type quiz, but more tailored to an individual person. In other words, differentiated. For instance, according to the Facebook world of personality quizzes, I am the following:

♦ Water (What element are you?)

♦ Viola (What Shakespeare character are you?)

♦ A Hobbit (What *Lord of the Rings* race are you?)

♦ Prof. Lupin (What *Harry Potter* character are you?)

These quizzes got me thinking. Maybe it would be worthwhile, from a student choice/student ownership point of view, to have students develop their own quizzes of sorts. Perhaps they can administer these quizzes to other students? Would that not add additional ownership towards reflection and give me additional information about who each of these students are inside? Furthermore, couldn't the quizzes also be another way to reinforce my subject matter?

The first thing I did was to have students gather their own information about characters from books they've read during the year: traits, internal conflicts, flaws, life themes, skills, etc. Then, they developed a kind of Facebookesque flowchart that allowed fellow students to follow a path toward a given answer. The student who authored the quiz provided a concise paragraph description of that character to distribute to students who qualify as that character.

So let's say the question is, "Which character from Gary Soto's *7th Grade* is most like you are now?" The student would go online to create a survey that ended with one of four character names: Victor, Michael, Theresa, or Mr. Bueller.

The student would also write a paragraph description of each character so that when a person's result was revealed, they could read the traits that most identify the character to the student who took the quiz.

Here are some programs that are available online to create quizzes for just this purpose:

- www.quiztron.com
- www.quibblo.com
- www.quizmoz.com
- www.gotoquiz.com
- www.proprofs.com/quiz-school

The creation of the quiz itself is a differentiated assessment of a student's content knowledge, and its cross-curricular assessment possibilities are endless:

- **Science:** What planet are you? (Applies science, mythology, and character traits to the planets.) Which inventor are you?
- **History:** Which monarch are you?
- **Math:** Which algorithm are you? (Assigns traits to different equations as well as understands the purposes behind their discoveries.)

The bottom line is that this isn't just some fun activity. All of this information ultimately helps me to help them learn. It begins with learning who we are as learners, learning who they are as learners, and helping them to learn themselves. From there, we can design targeted differentiated lessons to address their learning needs.

Designing Differentiated Lessons

When I'm designing a lesson that reflects my students, the three main questions I ask myself are:

- Who are my students?
- How should I deliver the material?
- What should I have them produce?

Assuming you already know who your students are (see section above), your lesson design homes in on the last two questions. Here are some quickie lessons that answer these very questions:

- **Lesson**—Decimal Placement
  - **Delivery:** *Kinesthetic*—Assign students to be the digits in a long number. Have them stand in order. Give another student a rubber band ball to be the decimal place. As the decimal student stands in different positions, have students in the class offer to "read" the number created.
  - **Product:** *Linguistic*—Have the students write out the numbers using words.
- Lesson—Westward Expansion
  - **Delivery:** *Visual*—Have students explore http://www.digitalhistory.uh.edu/ to view different maps representing the expansion.
  - **Product:** *Logical*—Create a map using coordinates like cartographers did so long ago.
- Lesson—Westward Expansion
  - **Delivery:** *Tactile/Kinesthetic*—Have students in groups literally "migrate" across the cafeteria, recreating the growth of our country.
  - **Product:** *Linguistic*—Write a narrative or dairy entry role playing the part of an early pioneer.

♦ **Lesson**—Writing an Expository Paragraph

  • **Delivery:** *Auditory*—Read aloud to the class an expository paragraph using a singsong voice. Use a high pitch for the main topic sentence, and as you progress towards the conclusion sentence, lower your register. Read the final sentence in a deep baritone.

  • **Product:** *Visual*—Have the students create a multilevel mobile of sentences that make up a paragraph of their own writing.

♦ **Lesson**—The Spread of the Roman Empire

  • **Delivery:** *Tactile/Kinesthetic*—Assign most students a country to represent and have them all stand in the correct position in the classroom as if they were a map. Instruct a student who wears the sign "Rome" on his or her chest to move around the tween map slaying other kids (countries) until he or she has conquered the classroom.

  • **Product:** *Natural*—Have the students bring in newspaper, website, or magazine articles about current countries who are expanding, threatening to expand, or who have already expanded. Ask if those countries are being challenged or accepted? Are they bettering the countries that they have absorbed or is the newer empire dissolving the native culture?

Of course, you can always give them choices, too. Choice is the ultimate form of differentiation. There's nothing more powerful. Offer them the choice to create a painting, act out a scene, or design their own assessment (see Chapter 7 for more on student-created assessments).

Student choice is also the ultimate in career and college preparation. Didn't you have decisions to make in choosing a career? Didn't you have a choice in where to go to college, what to study, and what to take?

We need to teach students to make wise choices, which can only happen by giving them different paths to go down or doors to open themselves. By giving students choice in what they produce as proof of their knowledge, you will get the most from them. You will perk up their engagement, which, in turn, leads to better classroom management. Just as importantly, the energy and excitement of students producing and achieving helps shake up the doldrums for you, the teacher, and an excited teacher, one that can't wait to see what his or her students have produced, is a teacher whose room is buzzing with every learning style.

10

Tips for Teaching Knowledge Through Questioning

Honor confusion.

— Sheridan Blau

I once had a student teacher who was conducting a lesson for my seventh grade class. I remember a student raising her hand and asking about the definition of theme. The student teacher identified it incorrectly, actually confusing the concept with simile. (Don't ask.) The kids who knew better began a classroom rumble that could have led to a Language Arts rebellion had I not interrupted politely and clarified; after all, we were doing some test preparation and the last thing these kids needed was to get their content derailed at this point in our preparation. Afterwards, I asked the teacher why he hadn't looked up to me for help or, better yet, asked the students. He answered, "I didn't know you could."

There is this misconception that a teacher needs to know it all. In elementary school, students think a teacher has the answers to everything. If that were the case, however, we wouldn't be model learners. By middle school they are convinced we don't know anything. The truth lies somewhere between. The fact is, not only don't we know it all, but we shouldn't even pretend that we do.

So fess up. Relax. It's liberating. OK, it's more than that; it actually models two key steps that are really vital for middle schoolers to know:

- Acknowledging and showing appropriate confusion

- Teaching how to question deeply

Frontloading these steps through your own modeling and strategic lesson planning leads to being able to seek answers comfortably.

There is a fear that if a teacher admits his or her own confusion, somehow the room of tweens would get downright ornery because they sense a weakness of authority in the classroom. However, there's a difference between having authority and being an authority. You can be the former and have control in the classroom without always being the latter.

The key is to teach in such a way that being confused is not seen as a weakness, but as a starting off point toward wisdom. Consequently, we must teach appropriate confusion. And this actually starts, as everything does, with modeling it.

Acknowledging and Showing Appropriate Confusion

Expecting tweens to show appropriate confusion begins by modeling your own. If we want to ween them off the eye roll, then we have to model how to be appropriate when we ourselves don't understand something. The eye roll is this additional commentary that comes from insecurity. Consequently, we have to show how to ask questions in a way that makes people think, not growl. It starts with our being secure in our not knowing.

Sometimes all it takes is not answering a great question, giving the silent "I don't know" it's time and letting the question lay there in respect, like when a student asks a question that is so deep, so great, that it stops time in a classroom and makes everyone think in one silent sigh. Not every silence requires an immediate answer to end. It is the silence that allows for thought. Taking that a step farther, by not answering the question, you have allowed possibilities to exist in student problem solving.

Being a lifelong learner starts with admitting that you don't have the answers to everything, and that admission allows for a student to perhaps fill the silence with his or her knowledge, giving that tween ownership in the classroom's learning process.

Continue to be a student and you will model how to take criticism and advice, which, in turn, earns you more respect from the students and ultimately leads to greater, more intrinsic, classroom authority. Admit when you're confused. Reflect verbally. Muse about your own failings and how to improve them. Purposefully pick up a dictionary in front of the kids to look up a word that confuses you. Ask a student for advice in front of the class. You will see the students begin to mimic these strategies as well, and with that will be a greater willingness from them to learn more.

So do yourself a favor. Give yourself a break. Admit that you don't know it all. Say it with a shrug. Wait, better yet, say it with words. In fact, have a script prepared. You can say…

- ♦ "I'm not sure. Let's ask a peer."

- ♦ "Well, why don't you hop over to the computer and let's find that answer."

- ◆ "What's the evidence prove?"

- ◆ "Dunno. What do you think?"

The power of being able to say, "I don't know" opens up worlds. To find answers, to problem solve our path to knowledge, is the true learning power; and it all starts with identifying a problem, discovering an answer not yet known, and giving students the tools to solve it.

How to Question Deeply

There is no multiple-choice test in life. Nobody asks the mechanic, "Do you know when the first wrench was invented?" Instead, they say, "Can you find out what's wrong with my car?" Nobody is going to ask their doctor to list the pieces of a stethoscope, but somebody will say, "I've got this pain right here. Do you know what it is?" Nobody is going to ask their accountant for the definition of "account," but they will say, "Where the heck is my money?!"

Ultimately, the best way to prepare students to be able to answer the bigger questions in life is in training them to ask questions themselves. The real power here, of course, is in modeling and training students to not only be comfortable by not knowing an answer, but also to be comfortable while they flop around trying to solve it. Problem solving is, after all, a messy business. In his amazing BBC documentary, *The Ascent of Man*, Dr. Jacob Bronowski states, "It is important that students bring a certain ragamuffin, barefoot, irreverence to their studies; they are not here to worship what is known, but to question it." Therefore, be tolerant of student mistakes and praise eloquent confusion, pointing out the intelligence behind certain errors.

> *Ultimately, the best way to prepare students to be able to answer the bigger questions in life is in training them to ask questions themselves.*

In fact, well-stated, well-thought out confusion is evidence of comprehension. Educator and author Sheridan Blau goes so far as to say that, "Confusion represents an advanced stage of understanding." It's not about what they already know, but about how they plan to answer their own inquiries.

Appreciating confusion isn't enough, however; a teacher needs to provide scaffolded tools to promote appropriate questioning. Because tweens think they know everything, they need the high-level tools to admit when they don't or they lose clout, either among their peers or, more often and more importantly, among themselves. Strategically teaching these tools will allow a student to save face because they will be drawing on academic strategies to show confusion; and this leads to deeper discussions about your content.

Begin by becoming accustomed to answering questions with questions. Use particular sentence stems and levels of questioning to model inquiry. Asking questions is, after all, the first step in launching that expedition to find the answers. Become familiar with adapting "This means" questions to "What if…" questions.

The six traditional steps of Bloom's Taxonomy represent a movement from the simplest questions to the most thoughtful questions. Asking "How would you define the water cycle?" is, after all, less rigorous than, "How would you generate a plan to produce energy from the water cycle?" Without even purposefully teaching the skills of questioning, you can use Bloom's in your own questioning to begin launching those expeditions. For instance, some sentence stems are:

- What alternatives would you suggest for…?
- Predict the outcome if….
- How would you compile the facts to investigate…?
- What criteria would you use to assess…?
- What choice would you have made…?
- How would you grade…?
- What explanation do you have for…?
- How is _____ connected to _____…?
- What are the pros and cons of…?
- What can you infer about…?

Now, with frequent use by the teacher, these strategies begin to lead into the student language as well. It's like osmosis. If they hear it enough, they absorb its purpose and will begin to use stems themselves like these with more frequency. These become a universal language in the classroom. A student who uses any of these stems clearly requires an awareness of the subject, almost as much as the student who responds. However, not all questions are created equal, so you have to move beyond simple modeling to more specific, targeted teaching.

After all, a question is a question is a question—right? Wrong! There are, as I'm sure you already know from your own experiences with students, good questions and bad questions. Now, don't give me that old line of "There are no stupid questions." Of course there are, and if we aren't helping students to understand the difference between a low-level and a high-level question, then we are totally to blame for the mass of ridiculous ones.

In the following lesson, I begin by introducing students to Costa's Levels of Questioning. Costa's is, in a nutshell, a more staccato version of Bloom's, making it more accessible to more students. Rather than talk using a vocabulary of six categories of learning, we muscle it down to three.

To begin, I always reiterate with my students that their brain is a muscle, and like any muscle, it needs to be worked out to stay fit. School, I explain, is our gym. "Now," I say, "if I lift a two-pound weight, will my muscle grow quickly and with tons of strength?" At this point I generally reach for a minor barbell that I keep handy for just such an occasion.

> *I always reiterate with my students that their brain is a muscle, and like any muscle, it needs to be worked out to stay fit.*

The catcalls typically answer me with such phrases as, "No way!" and "Weak!"

"OK, but what if I work out my muscle with a twenty-five-pound weight?" I reach for a bigger barbell that is kept under my desk for this demonstration. This is generally met with the occasional, "I wanna try!" and "Let me!"

"OK," I continue. "Would you all then agree, that there are activities that work your brain more rigorously then others? And would you also agree that when a brain is worked out hard, it might produce deeper knowledge than it did when it wasn't being challenged so much? And would you further agree that there are even different levels of questions, different quality of questions that, in fact, also work out your brain better than others?" I then talk to them about showing intelligent confusion, much as I have already described to you, as a means to prove just how much we comprehend a topic.

"For that reason," I continue, "we will be looking at the different ways to ask questions, and we'll decide if they are working out our brains just a little bit or working out our brains in a way that makes them sweat."

This is when I tell them about Costa's Levels of Questioning:

- ♦ **Level I: Input**—I start by reciting something. If it's eighth grade, I recite the *Preamble* to the Constitution of the United States; if it's seventh grade, I recite Shakespeare's "All the World's a Stage."

  "Reciting takes a certain level of skill, don't you think?" I ask, flexing my wrists like I'm working them out with the two-pound barbell. They nod. "But has it proven that I understand what I'm saying? Would you agree that proving that I get what's coming out of my mouth might work out my brain further?"

  Questions that are level one include sentence stems that ask them to: Recite, Define, Describe, List, etc.

- ♦ **Level II: Process**—I then recite my piece again, this time with inflection and passion, punching words verbally that are important and using my face and gestures to highlight the meaning of the words.

"Now," I say, "if I were to take apart these phrases and shuffle them around, say, in sentence strips on your desk, and you were to use the words and punctuation and meaning as context clues to put them back in order, wouldn't you say that you were working out your brain more than you did before?" This time I pick up the bigger hand weights. They start to nod more, some of them moving their arms too, some showing me their biceps, knowing what's coming.

Questions that are level two include sentence stems that ask them to: Infer, Compare/Contrast, Sequence, Categorize, etc.

♦ **Level III: Output**—"Now let's say I were to ask you the following question:

'Using textual evidence, could you predict what would have been the message of the *Preamble* if our forefathers hadn't used the word *perfect* to describe our union? How would the ideal of our country have changed if they had used the word *acceptable*?'

or

'Do you agree with Shakespeare that people have seven ages during their lifetime?'

...would you agree that now your brain is starting to sweat just a little?" I then reach under my desk for a 100-pound barbell that the class hasn't seen before. Incidentally, I'm a weakling. I can't lift it so well. Ah well, it's always good for a laugh.

Questions that are level three include sentence stems that ask them to: Judge, Evaluate, Create, Hypothesize, Predict, etc.

To put their knowledge into action, I then show them, via PowerPoint or previously made chart, the words and sentence stems to help them form their own questions for each of the levels, much like the list of Bloom's sentence stems above.

I follow this lesson with an assignment that assesses their ability to ask questions:

"Now, here's your challenge: You guys are creating next Tuesday's quiz for your fellow students on our latest reading selection. I want you to develop questions, high-level and deep-thinking questions. Show me how much you understand about your story by asking great questions." (See Chapter 7 for an example of one such quiz.)

Each student then creates ten questions of varying format, each using Costa's Levels of Questions. I cull through them, pick the ones I like, and—voila!—I have a student-created assessment that also assesses the students who created it.

I also like assessing questions using rubrics. Consequently, I've been working on developing a more formal rubric for students that can help them gauge for themselves whether a question they ask is high or low level. After all, providing them with sentence stems is only a scaffold. We eventually want to encourage them to try different stems of their own creations, to have the courage to question in ways that stray from our previous guidance.

Figure 10.1 is my work-in-progress rubric based on my own levels one, two, and three. I say "work in progress" because, let's face it, everything in teaching is a work in progress. As you'll see, the students must enter their question that is being assessed, break down it's true purpose, rank it, and give suggestions as to where to find the answer. They are ranked based on the number of brains it might take to answer the question, three brains being highest. Basically, a question that requires three brains might:

- Instigate discussion, even triggering more questions in its attempt to solve it.

- Require a hunt towards the solution.

- Produce evidence from the students.

- Expect students to support their conclusions.

- Bring in connections from other experiences or mediums.

Remember, you can assess students on not just about what they know, but also about what they *don't* know. If we wish for students to be curious in life, we must celebrate the dark matter between the spaces of their knowledge.

> *Remember, you can assess students on not just about what they know, but also about what they don't know.*

Good luck in your celebration, and with luck, those tweens will ask you a question someday so advanced in its comprehension of a subject, that you can honestly scratch your head and say, "I don't know; let's find out together." In the end, how you help guide that student to unlock that answer will be the real lesson learned.

Figure 10.1. Questioning Rubric

State the Question	Purpose of the Question…?	One Brain—I'm asking a question I already know the answer to	Two Brains—I bet with a little thought, we could answer this in no time	Three Brains—I don't know, but I'm going to find out!
Where can I find another word for plot?	Find a synonym	√ I can look in my textbook glossary or thesaurus		
Why did the Roman Empire last so long?	Analyze their success			√ I can look in my textbook, www.timelines.com or even ask my peers — Wasn't there an HBO show called ROME? Would that be something to rent?
Which came first: the Mac or the PC?	Sequence of Events		√ I can use an advanced Google search or wikipedia to find this answer	

11

Tips for Speaking Their Language Through the Use of Social Media

Evolution is evolution—and it's happened before us and will continue after we're gone. But what's taking place now is much more than change for the sake of change. The socialization of content creation, consumption, and participation is hastening the metamorphosis that transforms everyday people into participants of a powerful and valuable media literate society.

— Brian Solis

Imagine if society gave kids cars with no driving lessons. Imagine if society gave students access to the most miraculous library with no instructions about where to find the book they most wanted to read. So it is with social media and our students.

There are two Ts that are a magic bullet in educating tweens: talking and technology. Social media is the powerful tool that combines them both. Social media is generally defined as anything based online that is used in creating or cocreating through collaboration, sharing, and discussing information with others. Typically, using social media results in a product, maybe something that is read or can be viewed; and tweens eat it up.

Many people think of social media as merely used for the sharing of gossip and other informal purposes, perhaps using Facebook or MySpace just to name two. However, the term actually embraces a larger number of programs like Twitter, Skype, Ning, Scribd, Kidblog, Digg, and YouTube.

The fact is, if you have an interest, you can find a social network based on it. Many of your students may already have. In fact, according to the Pew Research Center, more than 72% of tweens and teens use some form of social media, and considering how much it is in use, there are two main reasons why we should be using social media in our classrooms for the sake of student achievement:

1. The kids are using it anyway, but poorly. Without our voices to guide them they are using it in a way that can cause their future and their reputations harm.

2. The world is using it outside of the classroom, and the skills we teach inside school must remain applicable to the world outside of school.

Despite this digital evolution, social media is a magic tween tool that many teachers and districts distrust and disallow. Perhaps it is a result of the stories of its abuse. Perhaps it is because of the potential for bullying or misuse some few have chosen to use it for. To combat its misuse I start by telling my students the following quote by online community manager, Erin Bury: "Don't say anything online that you wouldn't want plastered on a billboard with your face on it."

From there, I develop contracts, constitutions, and norms for how to behave both offline and online that can be backed up by consequences at school or even beyond. Be honest with students about the potential for irrevocable damage and they are more likely to respect the process. Unless we stake a claim in our students' education, they won't understand that fact fully. It takes a certain level of literacy and educational voice to participate safely online. That's where we come in.

Whatever the reasons to avoid using social media, they are not enough to actively create a gap that is ever growing between those who are engaging online (students) and those who are not (schools). Our distrust, I fear, is self-inflicted. By not using and modeling social media in schools, we are encouraging its abuse. By denying tweens this language in our schools, we are limiting their success in the future.

> *By denying tweens this language in our schools, we are limiting their success in the future.*

Furthermore, those who are creating a force online are innovative problem solvers. They are persistent. They know how to write. These are the skills that students need to have in school now, and the skills they will need to survive online long after the school bell rings.

Clearly, our students cannot be left out of this evolution. So this chapter discusses these topics:

♦ The Power of Social Media

♦ Teaching Internet Literacy

♦ Teaching Social Media Offline

The Power of Social Media

When I bought my most recent car, I first went online to look at consumer reviews and get input from other shoppers. My son's preschool recently launched a Facebook ad to connect friends of users to their website. Each night I check out Digg to see the new articles that are trending, based not on what the Associated Press deems worthy, but on the news that the public rank as the most important or interesting.

Many adults already use these tools in their own personal lives and even to fill in some professional gaps. Many of us use Facebook, which, as of 2010, was the third largest populated "country" in the world. Facebook's Baby Boomer population grew 107% between 2008 and 2009. Many of us use Twitter, which currently ranks twice the size of Greece. Many of us attend online conferences or gatherings, yet still there are many teachers, parents, and administrators who continue to struggle to make that leap to allow tweens to use these tools in education.

Yet using social media is not about learning the latest piece of fad equipment or taking time out of your curriculum to teach technology. It's about adopting a philosophy of allowing broad social interaction to teach your specific content.

- It's about teaching American history through unleashing your class to participate in TwHistory's Twitter feed. This interactive Twitter activity allows students to reenact such historical events as the Battle of Gettysburg through real time tweets with students in other states.

- It's about teaching science through having small groups present their DNA projects using Prezis (www.prezis.com) rather than a poster, and then posting those on YouTube for other classes to learn from.

- It's about teaching language arts through conducting book clubs using an online program such as www.kidblog.org to enhance your reading circles in the classroom and to continue the conversation long after the bell rings at the end of the school day.

Besides, it's just undeniably engaging. If you've ever found yourself befriending someone who has just discovered Facebook or Twitter for the first time or who just set up their first free WordPress blogging template for their own online diary, you know that their posts have the enthusiasm of a recently born foal on the first spring day. So it is with tweens who have just been exposed to blogging or voice thread or video conferencing.

When I first began blogging with my students, I was stunned that by the third day I had more than 800 peer-to-peer comments, some from students who had never previously raised their hand in class. The magic of their enthusiasm for the tool stunned me into social media submission.

It is easy and accessible now to be able to experience being published and read. The achievement gap is not just about content knowledge, but also about life experiences, and in this case, digital experiences are ever growing. As Seth Godin from Seth's Blog states, "How can you squander even one more day not taking advantage of the greatest shifts of our generation? How dare you settle for less when the world has made it so easy for you to be remarkable?" We cannot squander the opportunity to prepare our students for that world.

If you haven't already, I want to encourage you to enter into the world of social media itself. In fact, I challenge you, if you don't have one already, to open a Twitter account or a Facebook account. Find some friends to follow from both your school or wider profession and from your outside life. Toss in some family members, too. Update occasionally about what you're doing and what you've learned throughout your day. Based on your network of followers and those you follow, make a list of what comes your way that is positive. How does it enhance your life and your knowledge?

When I first thought about joining Facebook, my father warned me it was only for people who wanted to reconnect with their exes from high school. I had rolled my eyes like a tween again. Nevertheless, I joined anyway (so has he since then), and I discovered that, for me, the true benefit of Facebook is that it has rippled out my social and professional circle in ways that are immensely valuable. I found witnesses from different chapters of my life I would not have retained otherwise. Sure, once you join, you become inundated with photos of new babies, comments about friends' recent bodily functions, quiz results, and mysterious requests for farm equipment, but beyond the posts I saw that made me laugh, cry, and wince, I soon learned that Facebook was also a place of professional learning and development.

> *Once you join, you become inundated with photos of new babies, comments about friends' recent bodily functions, quiz results, and mysterious requests for farm equipment...*

But the power of using social media is, as I have said, one that should be used with our students as well. For instance, there's Tucson-based science teacher Brian Keivit and his Facebook fan page, Buffelgrass Shall Perish. The project was, he admits with a smile via Skype, "100% student created." In true problem-based learning format, this enthusiastic science teacher asked a group of eighth graders at his school to pick a problem in their local community and solve it.

They picked Buffelgrass, that fast-growing, flame resistant menace that is cheaply imported by some states as inexpensive erosion control and cattle feed. However, like something out of a B-horror film, it devours the natural habitat, stealing water and sucking the nutrients from the ecosystem, and has a shelf life seemingly longer than a Hostess treat. In other words, after we're dead and gone, Twinkies, cockroaches, and Buffelgrass will still be going strong.

Once the students discovered the plague-like weed, they weren't sure how to spread the word of its horrors. They decided to create a Facebook page devoted to the threat and soon posted a rap song on YouTube to educate the nation about this ground cover of evil. Using the social networking tools of our age, Kievit and his small group of students began to educate politicians, farmers, and Facebook fans like me. Using twenty-first century tools, they have become advocates for their own local community.

Yet the power of using these tools does not always have to result in policy reform in order to teach life skills. Its results can be far simpler and more resonating for the individual student, for using social media outlets can accomplish many of our goals we have been discussing throughout this book.

Using these tools taps into the skills for their future (see more on this in Chapter 5):

- ◆ Collaborating

- ◆ Communicating through writing

- ◆ Persuading

- ◆ Summarizing

- ◆ Using critical thinking skills

- ◆ Problem solving

As I have said, using these tools makes for engaging lessons that tap into students' need to talk to one another, creating better buy-in and an excited buzz to be there. Your structure combined with these tools makes for a well-managed classroom and one that refuses to be lost in an antiquated skill set.

However, just because students may be participating in social media already, does not mean they have the knowledge to participate in a rigorous way. You have to preteach how to function appropriately online before allowing them the freedom to communicate in that format. This takes teaching them lessons in Internet literacy, as well as creating offline versions of the online social media activities in order to establish your standards and expectations.

Teaching Internet Literacy

To me, Internet literacy is its own genre of reading and writing. After all, we can't assume a student who can rattle off every character from *The Lord of the Rings* can also read TiVo instructions with the same amount of comprehension. We also can't assume that just because a student can read print books deeply that he can also read online just as well. It takes specific, scaffolded lessons to accomplish, but not ones that stray too far from that which many of us teach already.

For the most part, to have good Internet literacy requires the skills many of us already work into our lessons. To have good Internet literacy, students must have basic reading skills, understand informational text, and comprehend visual literacy. They must be able to participate in multiple genres of reading and writing, must be able to segregate ideas into different layers with every page opened, and must be able to use quick-fire critical thinking and problem solving. In addition, they must have an understanding of social interaction through writing.

To teach to these skills, I break down the lessons into four categories: How to Read a Website; How to Research Safely; How to Write and Collaborate Online; and How to Use Proper Netiquette. To find out more about these and other categories of Internet literacy, check out Common Sense Media at http://cybersmartcurriculum.org/ for activities and lessons to further educate yourself and your students. Below are some lessons that I developed for my own classroom, as well as some key handouts from a workbook I wrote for Teacher Created Resources on the subject. Here are examples of lessons that address each of these goals:

1. How to Read a Website:

- Show students a website and have them identify the parts of the site. Give them the vocabulary that identifies each part (menu bar, banner, tab, etc.)

- Introduce students to the concept of three-dimensional reading. Have them explore an entire site by clicking from the home page to each of its menu pages and from the menu pages to pages beyond those. Have them discover the layers of a site and create a tally of the pages for the website without clicking away from that actual site. Your school's own website would be a great place to start this kind of project.

- Ask students to skim a particular site, so that they disseminate information quickly rather than reading each and every word. Skimming is a skill that is necessary when reading online because the visual and textual information can be so inundating. A student must decide quickly whether they are on a site that is biased or sponsored and should be discarded quickly, or beneficial and should be read more thoroughly.

- Explore www.amazon.com as the world's largest mall. Have them explore the page for a particular book that they may be interested in reading. Have them explore the author page, the sidebar menu of other genres, the bibliographic information, the books others recommend, etc.

2. How to Research Safely:

- Introduce students to the Advanced Google Search that allows a more detailed description of what a student may be looking for. The more detailed the search, the fewer of the pages that come back as possibilities, the more accurate the findings, the safer the results.

- Teach them to be Internet Detectives (Figure 11.1):

- Help students to cite websites appropriately. Two great resources for this are www.bibme.org and www.easybib.com.

- Have your class create a growing list of student-friendly websites that all students can refer to easily throughout the year.

- For your own education and professional development, check out Alan November and www.novemberlearning.org. November is the guru of educational resources on these subjects. He provides lesson plans and learning guides, and if you ever get the opportunity to see him present, don't pass it up. You won't regret it.

3. How to Write and Collaborate Online:

- Blogging: Create blogs that model and encourage a high-level of social interaction, interactions with guided eloquence. I use www.kidblog.org, which is a safe network that allows you to set up classes and discussion threads within five minutes of having made your decision to use it. It's amazing the freedom that blogging gives students to express themselves. Teach them how to comment on a blog, the standards of which must correspond to the rules of praise and criticism you expect in your own classroom (Figure 11.2, page 141).

In addition to providing this handout of general rules, I would also specify ahead of time the quality of comment that you expect. Model it by commenting first on a student post so that students can then follow suit. Provide guided questions so that they don't have to start with a blank brain.

(Text continues on page 142.)

Figure 11.1. Being an Internet Detective Handout

Being An Internet Detective: The Six Accuracy Steps Handout

The best part of the Internet is also the most suspicious part: the fact that anyone can write anything. The Internet is exciting because you have access to experts and information that your parents and grandparents never had access to. You can take a college level class, you can study any subject you want, and you can find the answers to almost anything. But it also means that anyone can put up a website that is false or misleading, and you don't want to fall for it.

Computers may be fast, but they aren't smart. That's where you come in. You need to check websites for accuracy before you use their information as fact. Here are six steps to check for accuracy:

☐ **Use Your Common Sense**

Ask questions. Asking questions is a sure sign of how smart you are. As you read website content, make sure you always ask yourself the following questions:

- Who is the author of this site?
- Is there evidence to support what the author is saying?
- Is there evidence somewhere that supports or disagrees with this author?
- Is this author biased?

☐ **Verify the Evidence**

Be a detective with everything you read. The answers all lie in the evidence. Keep on the lookout for:

- proper nouns
- dates
- important keywords

Take this embedded information to a search engine (like Google) and find other believable references to back up your information.

☐ **Triangulate the Data**

Look at the word "triangulate." The prefix is "tri-," which means _____. What this means is that if you can't find three sources to back up your fact, then you can't really know for sure if your fact is credible or not. Read suspiciously!

Being An Internet Detective:
The Six Accuracy Steps Handout (cont.)

☐ **Follow the Links**

To where a page links is as important as what information is on that actual page. Click on the external links to find the next layer of information about the author and his or her intent. Perhaps you'll be linked to an encyclopedia entry (reliable link), or perhaps you'll be directed to an Amazon or Café Press product (unreliable link). Don't fall for a website that's really an elaborate ad to sell someone's product or point of view!

☐ **Analyze The URL**

This is by no means foolproof, but it is a place to start in verifying the accuracy of the site.

☐ **Check the Publisher**

If possible, use websites like **easywhois.com** to check the background on the site to help you answer some of the questions in your head.

By checking off your accuracy checklist, you will have diminished the chances that you have fallen for a false website or a website that is more promotional than fact.

Congratulations! You are now an Internet Detective.

Figure 11.2. How to Comment on a Blog Handout

Netiquette

Netiquette: How to Comment on a Blog *Offline*

Online reading is meant to be very interactive. While there are those students who click around reading this and that, there are many who also comment on what they read. In fact, commenting is not only accepted, it's encouraged. Remember that just as there are classroom rules for responding to someone's writing and ideas, there are rules online when you are responding to a blog post or article. Here are some of the rules:

1. **Don't say anything you wouldn't say in person.** Just because you can't see the author doesn't mean he or she doesn't have feelings.
2. **Don't hijack the discussion.** Stay on topic.
3. **Bring something new to the conversation.**
4. **Don't be a know-it-all smarty-pants.** If you have to correct somebody, be polite. And you don't always need to be the one to correct somebody. Think of it like class: if all the students corrected each other every time someone misspoke or mispronounced, nobody would feel comfortable speaking out loud. It's the same online. It's more important to focus on the deeper content when reading.
5. **Make your tone clear.** Try not to use humor or sarcasm; they don't always go over well, even if you are the best writer ever. Use emoticons or write what the audience might see at that moment (shrug) to communicate your message clearer.
6. **Don't write anonymously.**
7. **Cite your sources with links.** If you mention a resource, link the words to the resource or provide the website for others to refer to.
8. **Paste quotes into your comment field.** If you are commenting on a quote within the post, copy and paste the quote into your comment field and then comment on it below so that the readers don't have to scroll back up to the original article.
9. **Don't comment when you are emotional.** If you are angry with someone for posting something, calm down before writing something that could forever be accessed. A good rule is to give it a day and then return to the post. Maybe even write a draft of your comment and let it lie for 24 hours. You can always cut and paste it into the comment field if you still believe it represents you well.
10. **Don't fan a flash fire.** A flash fire is when someone says something inflammatory and then people jump on the bandwagon, fanning the flames even more. If you ever see it happening, don't jump in. If there is a moderator, let him or her know what's happening. That will defuse it even faster.

©Teacher Created Resources, Inc.

- Video Conferencing via Skype: Adapt the netiquette guidelines to also help you set up expectations of behavior and netiquette when using Skype. Remember that it's the tech tool combined with good preteaching practice that really makes social media such a powerful tool.

- Twitter Conversations: Use Twitter to help collaborate with classes in other rooms, on other sites, in other states. I want to reiterate some of my classroom management strategies when I use Twitter in the classroom. Remember, I always keep it transparent, on one computer hooked up to the LCD projector, so that I can always see who is contributing from my class and how. I have also in the past used "Twitter Captains," deserving students who act as the written voice for other students in the classroom.

- For further suggestions on programs to use in the classroom, check out Allen Webb and Robert Rozema's *Literature and the Web: Reading and Responding with New Technologies* (Heinemann, 2008).

4. How to Use Proper Netiquette:

- Teach students the basic rules of netiquette (Figure 11.3) that should also correspond to the rules of behavior you expect in your own classroom. Create guidelines with how to use proper netiquette, which should be no less specific nor no lower in standard then how you expect them to treat each other offline.

- Discuss ethics. Have the students read the government's official copyright law, which can be found at http://www.copyright.gov/fls/fl102.html. Create a quiz at surveymonkey.com or any number of quiz-creating websites and develop reading comprehension questions for them to answer using our laws.

- Allow students to use texting language in note taking. This opens up a fluid conversation about when it is appropriate to text and when it is only appropriate to use more formal, academic language. Give them the outlet.

We are preparing students for their future, and the future is social media. However, it's possible, in fact probable, that Facebook or Twitter or MySpace, etc., won't be around forever. But these lessons about responsible social interaction in an online environment are vital regardless of the forum in which you teach them.

Figure 11.3. Basic Rules of Netiquette

Netiquette

Basic Rules of Netiquette

Offline

"Netiquette" is the accepted word for online behavior. It refers to the expected manners that everyone should use when they are communicating on the Internet.

The following rules are important to remember when you are online:

1. **Treat others with courtesy and respect.** Don't be cruel. Just because you can't see a correspondent, doesn't mean he or she can't feel. Here's a good rule of thumb: if you won't say it to his or her face, then don't feel liberated to say it in writing. Also, bullying is bullying regardless of whether it is physically on the playground or written on a note, blog, or email. Remember that everything that is written online can be seen forever. Don't let your online footprint be one that shows evidence of cruelty.

2. **Don't use bad language.** Using bad language just proves you don't know how to say something well.

3. **Don't spread rumors or lies.** This is a form of bullying and is against the law (and can be enforced by the law, too). Use the Internet to spread information, not instigation. Words and writing are powerful. With the Internet, anyone has access to giving information and reading information. Treat that power with respect and don't abuse another person or your audience.

4. **DON'T SHOUT.** ALL CAPS = shouting. Use all caps sparingly, as you would a highlighter.

5. **Don't break the law.** Stealing from others isn't just impolite; it's illegal.

6. **Share your expertise.** The Internet allows people from all over the world to share their knowledge. It's hard to imagine a time when we couldn't just Google any answer. You also have an audience for what you can do well. There are people out there who want to know how to do something that you already know how to do. Share your knowledge.

Basic Rules of Netiquette *(cont.)*

7. **Lurk before you participate.** "Lurking" is a term for reading and exploring a site before writing a comment. Read thoroughly before participating in an online discussion or activity. Know your audience before they know you.

8. **Control flame wars.** "Flaming" happens when the fires of gossip get out of control and rapidly spread. Sometimes flame wars start because someone started a discussion without any thought of holding back his or her emotions, and had the intention to flame others. Sometimes a comment begins a flame war. Don't get caught up in it. Don't be the dry grass that helps the fire to burn out of control.

9. **Be forgiving.** Everyone's a newbie at sometime in his or her life. Everyone misspells occasionally or offends someone by accident because he or she hasn't perfected an email voice yet. Just remember that most people online are well intentioned and looking to communicate and learn. Let the small things pass, and pick your battles.

So whether you are blessed enough to have the opportunity to teach in a computer lab full of state-of-the-art computers, or you only have a one-computer classroom, or you lack any equipment at all, you still need to speak this language and teach these skills. It will be their future, even if it isn't your present. To do this, even if you don't have the state-of-the-art equipment, you must develop both offline and online lessons to make sure you are hitting these important standards.

Teaching Social Media Offline

Let's face it, some classes may not have the computers or the district approval to allow these resources to be used in their school. In fact, not all of us are comfortable yet with our own interactions in the online pool much less comfortable with teaching others to swim. But that doesn't make it any less important to teach.

In fact, I would recommend teaching social media offline before even jumping into an online network with your students. It allows you to model the standard you need to see in their entries and level of participation. It will also help to relieve any fear you might have of jumping in because it's all done in the classroom using the supplies and tools that you would normally use to teach collaborative work.

Despite your possible discomfort, lack of equipment, or district short-sightedness, it is still your job to prepare these students for their future; and communicating and collaborating online using social media is here to stay. Maybe it won't be the exact incarnation ten years from now as it is today, but you need to be able to give your students the tools they will need to conduct themselves online. You need to be their voice of maturity, guiding them to make good decisions.

You need to be their voice of maturity, guiding them to make good decisions.

So regardless of what you have access to, you can still dip your toe into the social media pool, and reap the benefits of developing engaging lessons, by recreating simulations of online environments. This gives you the opportunity to begin speaking the language in the classroom of responsible social media interaction even if you lack the equipment. All it takes is a little offline role playing of online skills.

Here are just some examples:

1. **Offline Blogging**—Set up a poster of an article for each table group. Depending on what subject you teach, the article can reflect any content area. Have the students use sticky notes, stuck together in a chain, one right after the other, commenting on either the article itself or the previous student's comment.

2. **Use the Current Copyright Law for Reading Comprehension—** Rather than have the students go online to read the copyright law, print it out and develop multiple-choice questions for them to answer like a standardized test. This becomes test prep on informational text as well as a lesson on Internet ethics.

3. **Tweeting Core Knowledge—**Create a chart of growing "tweets" (140 characters only) that reflect that day's lesson. It can be a theme of a short story, dialogue tweets between characters, a chronological list of a particular timeline in history, attempts at an equation. It's not that this hasn't been done before, but by calling it a Twitter feed, it adds a layer of twenty-first century language to our everyday lessons.

4. **Texting as Note Taking—**OK, I get a lot of flak about this, but I think texting is just fine sometimes. In fact, just as is the case with much of technology, we've seen it before. Not so long ago, texting was called shorthand; so let kids create texts for core knowledge note taking. Let them listen to you and others and document what they've heard in texting language. Let them translate a history chapter into text, or switch the activity around and prep a paragraph of a concept using texting language and have them translate it into academic, formal vocabulary. There's a place for everything.

5. **Creating an Offline Wiki—**Much like the offline blog, you can also recreate some of the benefits of an online wiki with supplies as simple as a poster and crayons. The small group must, let's say, write an essay or create a mathematical equation. For each change to the original text, the person must indicate their participation by using their own color to visually indicate that the revision came from them. They can cross out, whiteout and write over, add, etc; in the end, the multicolored final draft or agreed-upon answer will reflect the collaboration of multiple students.

If someone told me that social media tools were created by tweens, I would totally believe them. As we all know, the creators of Facebook itself were mere college students at the time of its inception, and the tools themselves are in still their infancy. However, just as with any tool, the ability to use it alone does not guarantee its proper use. So it is with social media. In fact, because of education's silence on the subject, the one guarantee is that our students do not know how to use it appropriately. However, use it they do, and education must become a voice in the standard of its use. There is a conversation in the bandwidth that surrounds us, and we must be a part of it.

12

Tips Dealing with the Grading and Feedback Masses

I like a teacher who gives you something to take home to think about besides homework.

— Jane Wagner

When I think back of my time as a middle schooler, the pattern of feedback and grading was a routine in wasted ink. I wrote an essay, I turned it in, and two weeks later I got it back, my mind already on something else. I skimmed through the red marks in the margins that corrected my errors, finally landing at the end to note the letter grade circled at the bottom. If I turned in a math assignment, the feedback was even less valuable. Sure it was returned the next day, but the red cross outs of the numbers I got wrong, the fraction at the bottom of the numbers right out of ten, and a little note saying something along the lines of "do over," gave me no indication of how to improve my work.

As a student, this model of grading and feedback didn't work for me. I have to admit, however, that as a teacher, I recognize where it comes from. I think that there are two main reasons why teachers still follow this model. One, because many teachers believe that grades and occasional notes in the margins are, in and of themselves, feedback from which a students should derive a lesson. Two, teachers need grades for their grade books as proof of their efforts.

As I've grown as a teacher, I've had two great eurekas about my own grading practice and feedback routines:

1. The more traditional model doesn't improve my students' understanding of the work.

2. The more traditional model cannot evolve with the increasing class sizes in today's schools without taking huge chunks out

of my quality of life. This is important to solve, because if I go crazy, it doesn't benefit anybody.

Frankly, I like having a life, and I realized early on that I'm not one of those awe-inspiring teachers that stays at school until 10:00 at night, getting to school at 6:00 AM clutching stacks of papers, still struggling to grade them in time for the first period bell. I know some teachers do that, great teachers, teachers I learn from daily, but it's not me. I also realized that if I want to continue teaching to the best of my ability, avoiding burnout before I feel I've done everything I came here to do, I needed to adjust my practice so that I could continue serving the students and myself.

I don't know how your desk looks after your classes hand things in by their due dates, but mine looks like a mountain range of stacks, and that's not including the hilly region of late papers that trickle in after the due date. In fact, I need to launch an expedition just to reach the top of the piles in order to grade them by the report card deadline. Think about it: thirty-six to forty-two kids per class, six periods a day. How does a new or veteran teacher handle the hours of grading that can amount to a second full-time job?

As our class sizes increase, the typical strategies for feedback and grading must also evolve. Yes, it is still our missive to provide advice and reasoning for scores and how to do better, but the ways in which we do that must adjust to the reality of our overflowing student body.

> **As our class sizes increase, the typical strategies for feedback and grading must also evolve.**

There are tips and tricks to this vital part of our practice that can help. It just takes shifting your focus and your purpose. This chapter discusses some of the tricks I've adopted in my own classroom to handle the workload, referencing tips developed by other educators as well. I also provide quick-and-easy templates for scoring and giving feedback that won't put a cramp in your hand. I talk about the following:

- My grade book as an open book
- Managing grading and feedback options

Remember that these are always-evolving topics. What works for me one year with one group of students might not work the next year with a different group of students. However, the advice in this chapter will help you reclaim some of your time outside of the classroom and make your time in the classroom more efficient and enjoyable.

My Grade Book as an Open Book

The place to begin shifting your philosophy about grading is, of course, your grade book. Grades may not be the most enlightening form of feedback to a student, but it's what many parents look at, and even some students stop at the bottom line of "What's my grade?" Consequently, it's important to have a healthy relationship with your grade book, one that doesn't drive your classroom pacing. This starts with understanding why you grade.

I believe that the middle school teacher's grade book should reflect two main ideas: quality and responsibility. For this reason, I follow three key rules:

1. I don't use zeros to indicate quality.

2. I accept late work.

3. I allow for do overs.

My grade book allows for all three of these. Here's why: My job is not to punish, but to get the best I can from the students, to put every card in their favor. Thus I give scores that help students gauge their level of work, but I won't use a zero to indicate poor work. After all, a zero on a 100-point scale is nigh impossible to come back from, and a zero earned early on in the quarter is enough to bring down any student's enthusiasm for improvement. Consequently, I never use zeros to indicate just how low the student produced. I might use 50%, which is still an F, but never a zero. Using the big "goose egg" as an incentive doesn't work; it sends the message of "no return."

A colleague of mine from The Teacher Leaders Network and cofounder of the Accomplished California Teachers (ACT ning), David Cohen, has worked to develop his own theories on grading that combine some of his thoughts with those of Robert Marzano's findings. Cohen says the following:

> I've never met a teacher using a 100-point scale (as I did for more than a decade), who could talk about the meanings of 20, 30, and 40. Zeros are so far from 80, 90, or 100, that using them creates an unfair drag on the student's grade. If a student has an F on the first assignment (50/100), the overall grade can get back into the B range (80–89) if the student can produce six Bs in a row (@ 85 points). If another student has a zero on the first assignment, it will take fifteen Bs in a row to reach the B range. In that scenario, the zero is essentially penalized 250% more than the F….[T]hat means you can have fifteen Bs in a row, and one zero gives you a C+ average….What's the purpose?

Of course, there is a time and place for everything, so even in my classroom I find a place for zero, but in this case it indicates "never seen it, despite my efforts." I use it to indicate a deadline that has never been met. After all,

I think accepting late work is vital because it allows for a student to regroup and move toward improvement.

I also believe in allowing a student to redo work, showing improvement and learning. Being able to revise one's previous work is an indicator to me of more long-term comprehension. Doesn't disallowing the opportunity to improve fly in the face of learning?

Depending on the dictates of your district, you need to fool around with what you can weigh in order to set up the students for success. For instance, my district dictates that 70% of my grades must be in assessment, 20% must be for classroom work, and no more than 10% designated for homework. Philosophically, however, I believe that some assessments should be formative and some assignments should reflect the ability to meet deadlines. Because a student should be able to improve and rebound from errors, my grade book looks something like this:

Classwork	20%
Homework Quality	10%
Test (district and classroom assessments)	25%
Quizzes (classroom assessments)	15%
Projects (classroom assessments)	15%
Deadline	10%
Preparation/Organization	5%

Working within the limits of my own district's rules, I can create a flexible grade book that permits for late work and improvement. The scenario could go this like:

Juan turns in his homework late. He has a zero in his Deadline grade for that assignment until he turns it in. He does it over the weekend, knowing that there is a consistent and equitable ding for turning in late work. He ends up with, say, a 3 out of 5 for Deadline. That grade now stays put and is static. However, his Homework Quality earned him a B. Because I know that my priority as a Language Arts teacher is to teach content, that B is dynamic. If he wants to go ahead and improve on that, I tell him to go for it; but along with the redo, he also has to turn in a reflection sheet that explains the changes he made so that I don't have to regrade the entire assignment.

Later in the quarter, Juan takes a quiz and scores a C–. I don't know why; in an ideal world, his quiz score should reflect the quality he's been turning in up until then, but maybe his girlfriend broke up with him during the passing period. These things happen. The good news is that he can work to improve that quiz score and complete a reflection sheet, but he must do it within a certain amount of time or the score stands.

Thus, Juan has not only avoided a zero, but he has opportunities to show me he's learning.

Yet, the district assessment is supposed to be summative, that is, I can't let students take it over for a new score. Sure I have an issue with this, but as they say, "them's the breaks." However, I can have students reflect on their scores and responses, analyze why they missed certain questions, what they would do differently the next time around, and I can count that for an additional Classwork score. That's almost weighed the same, and frankly, it's more valuable to the student for their overall learning.

We must create a comfortable culture of revision in the classroom (regardless of our subject matter), or all we've done is condone the students to "shrug and move on."

We must create a comfortable culture of revision in the classroom (regardless of our subject matter), or all we've done is condone the students to "shrug and move on," regardless of mastery. However, we can't add to our already mountainous workload, so we have to get creative.

Managing Grading and Feedback Options

If it's important enough to assign them, then it's important enough to acknowledge something about the assignment that a student can learn from. However, I'm sure you've done the math: six periods, thirty kids per period, let's say three graded assignments a week. Eek! How does a teacher keep up the feedback on 540 assignments a week? Well, for all you newer teachers out there, the one thing you can count on is what Carol Jago says in her book, *Papers, Papers Papers: An English Teacher's Survival Guide*, "with confidence comes speed." But let's face it, even the most confident of teachers struggles with the growing workload, so the key is to give your feedback in different formats. It keeps them alert to your message, and it keeps you from going out of your mind.

Developing different techniques for grading and feedback doesn't take a lot of prep; it doesn't take a lot of worry. It takes a shift in philosophy. It takes removing some of the authority from your shoulders and putting it squarely on theirs.

Here is a list of tips, some old, some new, that have helped me manage my grading and feedback masses. They also help make the feedback I give more absorbent and effective toward my students' overall learning:

1. **Preemptive Feedback**—I was joking around with my three-year-old son one day while watching him attempt a thorough teeth-brushing session. After he set his Thomas the Tank Engine toothbrush down, ready to run into his bedroom for books, I jokingly said, "I definitely give that a B at best." He paused. "What's best?" he asked.

"Oh, well, that would be an A, but a B is better than a C, so a B means that's pretty good, but let's still work on it." It immediately occurred to me that I'd prejudiced him already against certain letters in the alphabet, but I figured it was bound to happen sooner or later.

"What's a D?" he said, getting back up onto his little stepstool.

"A D means that you probably aren't trying the way I know you can. A D means you showed up to brush your teeth, but you really didn't do much of anything."

"Ooo, that's bad," he replied. Then he picked up his toothbrush again. "OK, momma, so what do I do to get an A?"

I won't bore you with my description of tooth brushing excellence. I figure, after all, that if you're reading this book, you've got that one covered. However, I will say that the whole conversation got me thinking that many students don't know how to ask this question. In fact, many teachers still do not let their students in on this great secret.

It's about rubrics, of course. And it's about having the students establish their own standards. I talked about using rubrics, in particular, student-created rubrics, in Chapter 7. I think it appropriate to reiterate that rubrics aren't just about summative feedback, "Here's how you did," they are also a sort of preemptive feedback, "Here's what you need to do."

2. **Only Focus Feedback on One Skill**—If you've just taught a particular skill, that's what you should be focusing on when looking at the recent assignment. I know there may be other mistakes, but did they absorb the one you are most focused on right now? Also, think about it from a student's point of view: If the feedback is to mean something to them, it would make a greater impact and be less defeating to see specific and targeted notes on a single topic than to see the bloody explosion of red pen all over the place.

3. **Only Focus Feedback on One Part of the Assignment**—Let's say that the student turned in an essay. Assuming that this isn't some huge summative assessment, and instead is one where the student is looking for an indication of what still needs to be done before it can be called a final draft, you can look at, say, the first paragraph and only mark up that one section of the piece. If you're a math teacher, perhaps you're only looking at the first five questions of an assignment to give more detailed feedback about what the student does or doesn't understand about the concept. Better yet, regardless of your subject, allow a student to choose the section or numbers they think best represent their comprehension. Then have the student take what they learned from the section about which you advised and try to apply that to the rest of the assignment.

4. **Rotate Students to Whom You Give Feedback**—Sure each student turns in the assignment, but do you really need to focus as intently on all 200 of them equitably every time? Rotate groups of students that get more percentage of your attention. For example, give in depth feedback to certain groupings of students, a focus group based on any chosen qualities (e.g., random, last name A-M, all odd identification numbers, levels) and skim over others, looking at only key components of the assignment.

   For gifted students who don't fall into that assignment's focus group, I may skim for über-thesaurus usage and overly elaborate sentence structure. For others, I skim for the basic building blocks of writing: thesis statement, transition words and phrases, quotes, main topic sentences. However, it's a skim until the time when they are included in the focus group, and their time comes around frequently.

5. **Train Students to Give Feedback to Each Other**—Using different formats like blogging (see Chapter 11) and peer-developed rubrics (see Chapter 7), train the students to give a first wave of feedback in the earlier stages of their learning. This not only saves you from having to repeatedly write the same basic comments that could have been easily caught by a peer, but it also trains them to know what you need to see, eliminating some of the errors in the first place.

6. **Comment Rather Than Correct**—Carol Jago says that we should "comment rather than correct," and she's dead-on right. It should be the students' job to correct their errors; however, it

would be more powerful for them to identify the errors in the first place.

Therefore, you can make your feedback a scavenger hunt of sorts by using some of the following sentence stems:

- In your essay, I see *(general mistake)* appear *x* number of times.

- In your history project, I see two date errors.

- In your math assignment, I see three equations that do not add up.

Remember that you want them to be paying attention to your advice. Keep them awake and alert to your guidance by making them work for it.

7. **Create Feedback Templates**—Don't waste time writing in words. Create templates with the most common errors based on your subject, unit, assignment, etc., as a checklist of sorts to use from year to year. Make rubrics that can be circled or high-lighted.

Develop surveys that can be bubbled in quickly.

I personally love the Project-Based Learning checklist website for creating rubrics for easy scoring and feedback. You can explore it at http://pblchecklist.4teachers.org/.

Checklists may not be the most powerful strategy visually, but they're quick to produce, quick to fill out, and easy to read. Besides, if you mix this strategy up with others, kids will respond to the variety.

8. **Create a Key of Feedback Symbols**—In the beginning of the year, identify the most common errors that you predict you will see. Then develop a quick key of symbols that you can use in the margins instead of writing in sentences or bullets. This will require the students to translate as well, which embeds the lesson even further.

As a Language Arts teacher, I tend to begin the year basing my symbols on the list from Jeff Anderson's *Mechanically Inclined* (Portland, ME: Stenhouse, 2005) and the "20 Most Common Used Errors." However, I also throw in some errors based on the students' benchmark essays. You can create a key of feedback symbols for any subject matter. Figure 12.1 is a list of symbols that I have used in the past.

Figure 12.1. Editing Feedback Symbols

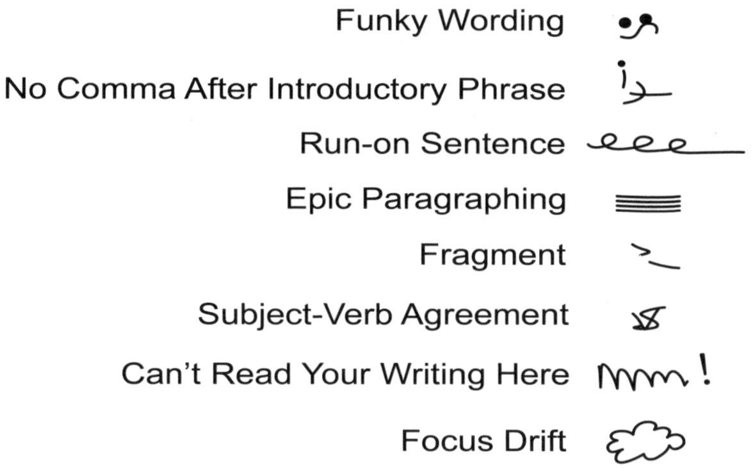

Funky Wording

No Comma After Introductory Phrase

Run-on Sentence

Epic Paragraphing

Fragment

Subject-Verb Agreement

Can't Read Your Writing Here

Focus Drift

9. **Grading Groups**—Get some folks together for a little grading fiesta. Have a potluck meal. A little food and a little conversation goes a long way toward making grading and giving feedback a less tremendous chore.

10. **Outsource the Grading**—Sometimes assignments will take a huge leap in quality when students think someone other than their own teacher is seeing them. Don't take it personally; it's about mixing up the feedback that a student gets. However, remember that it's only a special assignment that can get outsourced. You don't want to do it unless you really already know your students and their abilities. After all, collecting, giving feedback, and scoring are as much about them learning your content as it is about you learning about them. Here are a few outsourcing possibilities to consider:

- In Chapter 7, I mention that one of my end-of-the-year assessments is a persuasive letter pitching a new elective, and that it is actually graded by administrators, not by me. I collect the letters and distribute them, along with their corresponding rubrics, to willing administrators. This gives the students someone to write to, and it pulls from them a more authentic voice in the assignment. The administrators see the best and the worst from the class, sure, but they are involved in student learning.

- Switch assignments with other teachers just to mix it up. Some teachers will notice one skill, whereas others will home in on a different skill. The more eyes on a student's work, the better.

Inevitably, when students know that persons other than their teachers are grading them, they try to step it up a notch.

- Have a contest. Challenge another class to a content contest, and have a third-party class correct and evaluate the results. (See Chapter 2 for more on this.)

11. **Mix It Up**—Throughout the year, make sure that students have a variety of possible projects to turn in, and that the projects are interesting for you to grade. Let's face it, not every assignment has to be an essay or multiple-choice boringness. Sometimes have them present oral presentations that can be scored with a rubric right there on the spot. Have them present PowerPoints, reader's theater, etc. Nobody said you had to carry stacks of papers home every day for your scores to be valuable.

12. **Keep Them in Suspense**—Keep the final grade of an assignment as a carrot dangling until the feedback is read, absorbed, attempted, and proven. Make them solve some of the problems in the assignment based on your feedback, and trade their solutions for access to their score. Create steps to reach the information that they seek, almost like an academic scavenger hunt. For instance, on the day you return an assignment to your students, reveal (with great flourish I might add) the following cryptic message on the board:

"To see your score, you must accomplish three tasks:

1. Solve one of the problems I have posed for you in your individual assignment.

2. Pass your assignment to a peer and have them solve another issue that I have raised on your paper.

3. Read through an assignment carefully and find the mystery symbol I have embedded somewhere on your paper. When you have this symbol, and you have improved your work, you may come to me and whisper it as the secret password to get your final score."

Goofy, I know, but it gets them to read the entire piece using a different lens. It's fun, and it provides a level of play to an otherwise tedious task for both you and your students.

13. **Oral Feedback Sheet**—One day I was reading an assignment, correcting pen in hand, making notes in the margins. I was shaking out my cramping hand when I started asking myself, *How*

can I make my advice sticky, "gluing" it somehow to my students' consciousness in a way that my handwriting did not? Eventually I asked myself, *Why am I the one taking the notes? Is not the one who does the work, doing the learning?*

In response to these questions, I developed the Oral Feedback Sheet (Figure 12.2, page 158). It's a template for note taking that the student uses while in conference with the teacher. Sure, it takes up class time for the conference, but I've seen huge differences between those classes with whom I've made the time to do this activity, and those who have just received feedback via my notes to them.

Set a timer, sit down with each kid, and hand over the job of note taking while you give oral feedback. It takes class instructional time, but it's valuable one-on-one time, and the rest of the class can be revising or working on another lesson in the background, waiting their turn at bat. Just as importantly, however, the oral feedback sheet has proven to be more effective for me than traditional feedback, and it doesn't take time away from putting my own kid to bed at night.

It's not something I do every time. It's one of the many tools I use to keep giving feedback fresh for both my students and me.

14. **Reflection Sheets**—Earlier I noted that I allow students to improve on their scores, but they must include a reflection sheet of the steps they used or learned in order to prove their improved knowledge. By producing a reflection sheet, you don't have to go through the actual steps of rereading a student's work. Simply look at the recorded improvements and reflections to decide if the student's current grade stands or can be bumped up. (See Chapter 4 for a version of the reflection sheet I use.)

15. **Stagger Due Dates for Your Classes**—There is no rule that says all 200 shoeboxes or flipbooks have to show up at your door on the same date. You can assign Period 1 to turn them in on Monday, Period 2 on Wednesday, Period 3 on Thursday, and Period 6 on Friday. You'll only get pushback from the Period 1 students once, but when you explain that next time, a different period will get the first due date, the complaints will die down soon enough.

Sometimes, this strategy doesn't always work, and it can feel like the work coming in never ends. Then again, your piles aren't as tall, and you can chip away at the grading before the next barrage of projects appears.

Figure 12.2. Feedback Sheet

Own Your Own Feedback!

OK, I'm going to sit down with you to give feedback on your essay. During this meeting, you are to take notes to use as a reference later when you are revising or finalizing your paper.

THESIS STATEMENT NOTES: _____
_____
_____
_____

This is great, keep doing it, don't change a thing!	To be revised, considered, mulled over, overhauled

Based on the essay in front of me today, my teacher is giving me a *(enter grade)*.

Think about it: Am I satisfied with that? Y / N

Due date of Final Draft based on our discussion: _____

Signed: _____ Date: _____

16. **And while you're at it, give them a way to give feedback to you**—If they believe that you are reading their feedback, don't you think they will be more likely to read yours? Develop a template for them to fill out at the end of a unit, quarter, semester, whatever. Better yet, develop a survey on surveymonkey.com that allows them to give you quick feedback. Ask them what works and what doesn't, what lessons stuck and which ones didn't help at all. This will also help you develop more effective lessons for the following year so that you don't waste time with assignments and activities that aren't resonating with the students.

This creates more buy-in for their own reflection, and that translates to greater achievement. I end this chapter sharing my own survey (Figure 12.3, page 160), which I give to my students at the end of the school year. Once I read the responses, I compile some of them into a PowerPoint of advice to my incoming students about my expectations, more challenging units, and overall wackiness. In the fall, I show the presentation to my new students. That way, the voice of my exiting students can be still be heard resonating within the classroom, by the new community of tweens.

Figure 12.3. End-of-the-Year Survey

1. Approximately how many independent reading books did you read this school year? _____

2. What will be your greatest fears about moving to the high school? ___

   _____

   _____

3. What are the most important skills &/or strategies that you learned in Mrs. WG's class this year? _____

   _____

4. What is it that you are still frustrated by in Language Arts? _____

   _____

   _____

5. What was the most interesting lesson in this class this year? _____

   _____

   _____

6. What was the least interesting lesson in this class this year? _____

   _____

7. What would you like to see more of? _____

   _____

8. What was your favorite writing genre? Please circle:

   Narrative   Summary   Lit. Analysis   Persuasive

9. If you were a giving advice to an incoming 8th grader, what would you tell them about how to succeed in Mrs. WG's Language Arts class?

   _____

   _____

10. Will you come back and visit? (Don't answer that, just feel free to come by whenever you can and say hello.)

    Enjoy the adventure that is the next chapter of your life. High school gives you access to try out everything. Take advantage of it and take a bite out of everything. Good luck, remember your Courtesy Contract, and remember that there is a teacher in middle school who will miss you.

    Sincerely,

    Mrs. Wolpert-Gawron

13

Tips for Being Flexible

It is not the strongest of the species that survives, nor the most intelligent that survives; it is the one that is most adaptable to change.

— Charles Darwin

The most powerful tool for staying sane as a teacher of tweens is to be flexible. I know it can be difficult, especially when you're only give forty-five minutes to get through your lesson, and they're nuts from the fire alarm that just went off during last period, and the test is just around the corner. It sounds simple to do, but if there's one thing you can count on in education and in middle school, it's that you can't count on anything. Remain mentally supple and you'll accomplish a lot more in a much happier state.

There are a few ways to look at this advice, and this chapter discusses these topics:

- ◆ Be Flexible Because Education is an Ever-Evolving Entity
- ◆ Be Flexible Because Things Go Wrong All the Time
- ◆ Be Flexible Because It Makes for a Healthier and Happier You

Be Flexible Because Education is an Ever-Evolving Entity

Education changes. If you entered what you thought would be a static, once-I've-learned-it-it'll-never-change profession, boy, have you got it all wrong.

Our country's history in education can best be summed up by this word: unpredictable. From the time the first free school was opened in Virginia in 1635, education has seen its pendulum swing widely from year to year. From hickory sticks to timeouts, from repetition drills to critical-thinking skills, there have been countless strategies touted as being the silver bullet, only to mutate from decade to decade.

There's no single generation of teachers that has not been asked or required to adapt. In education, we see a metamorphosis in any of the following at any given time:

1. **Our Demographic**—What is the make up of the class in front of us this year?

2. **Our Students' Savvy Index**—What do they already know? With increased rigor starting earlier, after all, wouldn't they come in knowing more than they did last year?

3. **Our Short-Term Goal**—If it isn't a new set of standards, it's a list of new methodologies. If it isn't a new textbook, then it's a new program or administrator. If it isn't to meet this goal, then it's to meet another goal.

Consequently, we need to be flexible if we are to be as successful as we can in our job. Be prepared for the pressure that comes with the changing of the educational tides. Make sure you're open to the shifts when they occur, because sometimes they will actually improve your practice. Don't choose the wrong the battle to fight; that's counterproductive.

The best way to arm yourself in education is by preparing yourself. Prepare your heart and your brain by prioritizing what's being asked of you. Follow your gut, but don't dig your heels in when a fad clearly isn't going away.

Sometimes you should also ask flexibility of yourself. For instance, I would recommend being a part of a pilot group every once and awhile. It's important to try new methods and theories early on so you lessen your learning curve later. In addition, being part of a pilot group of some newly adopted equipment or curriculum also means others might be more focused on you and your training. Your flexibility early on might pay you back in the end, making your learning experience easier than had you waited for the new strategy to become a mandate. Also, by making sure that you always have some new element to your practice, you are, in turn, working out your ability to be more flexible when it is forced upon you.

The bottom line is this: prioritize for yourself. On the one hand, don't be the teacher who is still fighting differentiation and has created her very own professional achievement gap as an educator. Don't fight using technology in the classroom, thereby creating a reason for a school to seek out someone to fill your obsolete shoes. On the other hand, don't feel you have to jump and do everything. Take a breath and follow your instinct. Keep your goal in mind—teaching students—and do what speaks to that goal.

Be Flexible Because Things Go Wrong All the Time

Stuff happens. You've done everything right and still things go wrong. You welcome the guest speaker that will hook these kids into a life of success, and there's a fire drill just as he opens his mouth. You plan for that critical lesson that brings everything together before the next day's test and you get a call to send all your English Language Learner students to Room 6 for testing. You have the supplies out on the desks for a collaborative activity, but the drama from lunch walks into the room with the students in tow.

As a tween teacher, you have to be flexible. Just as the physical appearance of a tween morphs from day to day, so must your lesson plans. If you can ride with the waves of change, you decrease your stress and be open to quick ideas on the fly so that you lose less instructional time when lessons hit the fan.

> *Just as the physical appearance of a tween morphs from day to day, so must your lesson plans.*

Here are two examples of what I call Flexible Teaching. The first chronicles the story of a typical lesson gone horribly wrong. The second describes how I solved teaching with a case of laryngitis. Both involved the need to be flexible so that I didn't lose instructional time or get too stressed out about losing the time.

1. **The Case of the Missing Link**—In hindsight I've decided that it was clearly my excitement that doomed my lesson from the start. Allow me to elaborate.

   Days before beginning my narrative unit, I had my opening activity already bookmarked on my computer and ready to do. It was a poignant, three-minute amateur video that had all the marks of a great narrative. I was convinced that it would have the kids in tears by the end, and it would help set the tone for writing some serious stories. I was pumped.

   But this hyperbolic dream was not to be. Despite my prep work and my enthusiasm, I couldn't get the link to load. It was gone. That's right, between 7:45 AM and 8:15 AM, the link had disappeared into that place where single socks all reside: prep purgatory.

   However, because I knew that things go wrong, I reached for my Plan B. In this case, it was a narrative outline template in the shape of a story arc that I keep in a copied stack in the cabinets. At least it gave them something worthwhile to do while I tried to solve the link problem. The instructional time wasn't what I had planned, but it wasn't lost either.

2. **The Case of the Missing Voice**—One thing I can count on each year is my own laryngitis episode. It's not so bad that I feel I have to take a sick day, but it does make for a typically verbal-based job to be somewhat challenging. Now, I'm not talking about still whispering here. I'm talking about a totally stripped, honk-when-I-try-to-produce-sound lost voice. So knowing that it will happen at least once, I can be prepared to be flexible.

It's true. On those days when I've totally lost my voice, I still teach. Admittedly, it feels like someone has taken the hammer from my toolbox and still asked me to pound in a nail, but there are ways around losing your hammer.

In fact, sometimes, these days become really fun and really rigorous for the students. First off, it forces me to get creative. So here is my lesson plan for the mute teacher:

Turning in Homework: Now, I generally have a homework collection procedure in place, a location in the classroom for them to turn it in, but when I lose my voice, I want to still stress that I'm in charge and despite my lost tool, they can't get away with anything without my notice. I think it's important to mix things up a little on those days so that the students have to pay particular attention. Therefore, when my class walks in there is a large sign outside my door asking them to do the following:

1. Line up at the door.

2. Take out your homework. (This could be, for instance, an index card with the hook—the first few sentences or so—from their current reading book.) Fold it, and as you enter the room, please deposit it in the jar on the table in the back of the room.

3. If you don't have your card, write your name on the clipboard.

I stand by the door like Julie McCoy, Your Cruise Director, clipboard in hand, pointing silently with my voice, but loudly with my eyebrows. The kids, normally a rambunctious "I got here first!" kind of group, quietly file in and take their seats. Homework collected: check.

In the front of the room, using a combination of dramatic mime and sign language hastily remembered from some bygone day-camp activity (but quite useful for reasons such as these), I spell out who should get the journals and Works in Progress folders from the cabinets.

I then sit quietly in the front of the room with great drama and flourish and proceed to type on my computer that is hooked up to my LCD projector so that they all can see:

> OK, I've lost my voice. But this does not mean this is a recess period. Please take out the Rough Drafts of your latest Narrative. Stick our your tongue if you've read this direction.

The class pretty much then happens as any other class does. I type directions, they follow them. I'm still monitoring and showing them I haven't lost my classroom management savvy, and they are actually focused and can't wait to see what I have to type. I continue:

> OK, some authors are inspired by a character. We'll work on that next week. Some authors are inspired by themes, a moral, a message that they need, must, just *have to* get out there to their readers. We'll be talking further about that, too. Jose, go throw out your gum. Some are inspired by hooks. Let's look at a hook from a professional writer and begin a narrative using that Hook....

Teaching doesn't require volume. Classroom management doesn't require yelling. Being in control is about humor, it's about having your antennae up, and it's about being creative enough to make every moment valuable. Teach your kids to make the best out of any situation and you will have taught them a lesson greater than the one dictated by the standards.

I should note at this time that I don't always have a plan B for every lesson. To be honest, I'm not that organized. I do, however, keep an emergency substitute plan in the box under my desk, copies already made in case I drop with Ebola or something. Just remember that if you end up using your emergency lesson, replenish it, so that you aren't hit with a double emergency: Ebola and no copies.

For instance, let's say you woke up late, you spilled your coffee all over your pants, you got to school only to discover that you have Individualized Educatin Plan meetings scheduled during two periods, and now you need to make your students' time worthwhile. What do you do? Well, here are just a few lessons you can have on hand for quick substitute or low-energy deployment. They can be used in any subject and can be go-tos when you hit the occasional curriculum wall.

1. Newspaper Scavenger Hunts—What you need:

- Scissors

- Stack of newspapers (keep a box on hand or ask the office for some)

- List of elements to hunt for (kept on hand for just such an occasion)

Now, depending on the subject you teach, you can have the students find and cut out anything from weather reports to book reviews. Have them seek out fractions, decimals, information on the planets, or information on a country. The ability to read and comprehend informational texts is required of all standardized tests, and the activity itself uses a variety of modalities. You don't have to feel guilty about using this activity as a fallback—it's worthwhile. Have the students construct a poster of examples for your Content in Context Display (see Chapter 1 for more on this display) in their small groups.

2. Visual Note Taking—What you need:

- Paper

- Pens or pencils

- The textbook or any assigned reading material

This one is all about nonlinguistic representation. Assign a chapter in the book for them to reread as a review. The activity is that they must take notes on the chapter, but there is one rule: no words allowed. They may only use numbers, pictures, icons, and symbols to convey the meaning of the chapter or unit.

3. Texting as Note-taking—

- Paper

- Pen or pencil

- The textbook or any assigned material

I talked a little about this in Chapter 11, but I believe that there is a place for texting in the classroom. Have the students translate a passage or chapter into texting language. Have them create a key of new symbols from the standard QWERTY keyboard to represent the content in the classroom. Then they can hand their notes to another student to have that student translate their texting back into a more academic language.

Remember, flexibility isn't just about creating a rigorous alternative when Plan A fails, but it's also about being more healthy and happy in your job too. It's OK to stray from your routine occasionally so long as your routine is well established and easy to get back to next time. Nothing's so irretrievable that it can't be bent a little, every once in a while.

Besides, being flexible is good for your own brain, too. You don't want a dry, crusty brain, incapable of new thought. You want a juicy, flexible brain, one that is able to move through the challenges of life. Change happens in life, and we have to be able to change with it.

Be Flexible Because It Makes for a Healthier Happier You

Being flexible isn't only about what's best for your students and your practice. It's also about being a happier teacher in a difficult job. Did you ever read about the nuns involved in the Alzheimer brain study, the School Sisters of Notre Dame? They appeared in *Time Magazine* some time ago, and occasionally my thoughts go to their story. They are an order of nuns who, as a means to continue giving back, have allowed scientists to track their aging brains over the decades, finally donating them for analysis upon their deaths. What scientists have learned from these women is remarkable. It seems that despite their ages of death, these nuns die with a great amount of cognitive agility still intact. They tend to keep diseases like Alzheimer's and dementia at bay, and even live longer than average, still maintaining, for the most part, active brains.

The studies found that their success was in part because of their ability to keep their brains flexible. That is, they used language, they did crossword puzzles, and they tried to keep a positive attitude. I also wasn't shocked to discover that of almost 700 patients and future donors, nine out of ten of the nuns had once been teachers.

Teaching is a job that demands flexibility. Being able to bend with life, being able to allow change to roll off your back with less anger, helps you not only do a better job, but also turns out to be better for you in the long run.

Flexibility is the key to teaching middle school.

This isn't just about being healthy, it's also about student achievement. Flexibility is the key to teaching middle school because it's modeling a skill these students must learn at a time in their life when they also crave the most constancy. Thus plan for something that you feel confident in, but be just as confident that things won't go as planned. Remember that there's only so much you can do to plan, and after that, your job is also to teach how to move on. Prepare these tweens for their lives beyond school, and flexibility will be a part of any career they pursue.

When the phone rings in the middle of class, when you're asked to substitute because a colleague went home sick, when the assembly is scheduled during your class yet again, don't see red. Calm down. Be flexible. It makes you a better role model. It makes you a happier teacher.

14

Tips for Publicizing Your Efforts to Get What You Need

Publicity is a great purifier because it sets in action the forces of public opinion, and in this country, public opinion controls the courses of the nation.

— Charles Evans Hughes

I know we wear a lot of hats already, but I believe that we teachers need to doff a new one, that of our own publicist. When you have good publicity, everything runs smoother for you. You hear "yes" more often, your students have more pride, and their pride trickles into greater achievement. They achieve more, things are easier for you—bada-bing, bada-bang—happier teacher.

Yet it doesn't stop there. Publicity and good reputations do not have a quota. One teacher who gets attention for his or her accomplishments does not need to preclude attention for another teacher. There is enough reputation to go around. In fact, once enough teachers on a staff commit to publicizing their efforts and successes, an entire school can change.

Why do middle schools need good publicity? Because no matter the district, it's the middle schools that have the wild reputation. There seems to be an avoidance of the age group all together, like a don't-look-at-the-tweens-behind-the-curtain kind of thing, leading to an inherent misunderstanding of tween teachers' efforts. A misunderstanding that the energy on a middle school campus can't possibly equal achievement.

The only way to counter these misunderstandings is through publicity. I'm not asking you to change how you teach or how you practice. I am encouraging you to change how you brag. I'll say it: Teachers need to become showoffs.

There are two key elements that dive deeper into the rationale of why you need to have some acuteness in publicity:

- ◆ Actively Publicizing

- ◆ Teaching with Your Door Open

Even though middle schools could use the good press, even in their own district, the fact is that a teacher of any level, be it elementary, middle, or high school, should learn how to pitch what's working in his or her classrooms, schools, and districts. It's up to you to learn how to get the best of what happens in any school out there so that the outside world doesn't come to its own conclusions.

Don't be intimidated. You know how to write persuasively. You know how to speak persuasively. Think of it as your own authentic assessment, your own project-based learning, and let the press be your friend.

Actively Publicizing

Let's get to the nitty-gritty and talk about different strategies of publicity. Early on in my teaching career, I discovered that there are elements to teaching that I love and elements that I don't love. The parts I love are the students, curriculum creation, life-long learning. The parts I don't, however, are the isolation and the negative reputation, and I hate feeling the victim. Consequently, I began reaching out in my voice and my writing. You can, too. Or if that's not for you, there are other ways to publicize the coolness that is happening in your classroom. After all, it doesn't matter the size of the pond, just be a respected member of it.

1. **Contact the Education Editor of Your Local Newspaper**—For teachers to reach out to the press, Beth Cleveland, of Elm Public Relations, broke it down into a series of steps that really highlight the initial prep work. In a nutshell, here's what to do:

   - Read. Read the periodicals (newspapers, newsletters, professional journals, magazines, online periodicals, etc.) that might jive with your idea for a story. Google News is another place to search. Do the groundwork, so you're not wasting someone's time, including your own.

   - Find out the name of the reporter or editor who is covering education for that print or online resource. They love a good story so long as it falls under what they tend to write about. So do your research.

   - Ask what their preferred contact method is: phone or e-mail.

   - Your verbal or written pitch should include or be the equivalent of a short essay. In other words, start with an opening sentence about why the reporter should care, why the story is important, or who the issue effects. From there include what amounts to be about two short paragraphs highlighting the most important or exciting facts about your story. End your pitch by sharing your contact information and your availability to talk further. Cleveland reminds us that "reporters prefer short, concise story pitches, and they will get in touch if they want more info." She also warns, however, to "Try not to overwhelm them with story ideas. Instead, be selective and send them story pitches that really sing to their interests."

In terms of what reporters find newsworthy, Cleveland highlights the following seven points:

- Impact
- Prominence
- Timeliness
- Proximity
- Controversy
- Uniqueness
- Emotion

2. **Write About Your Own Successes**—Blog. Write articles. Submit editorials. Regarding blogs, there are tons of free templates to use to just start up your own online diary of coolness. For instance, Google offers a great free blog that's simple to set up and simple to maintain. Wordpress is another one that is very popular and free. You might also try Blogspot, which many teachers and classrooms currently use.

3. **If You Don't Write, Find Someone Who Does**—Find someone who blogs and get them to profile some of what you're doing in the classroom. Share your successes. Get yourself out there.

4. **Get Thyself a Twitter Account**—Twitter is a free and easy social networking tool. It allows you to post in 140 characters or less what you're doing at any given time. Just had a breakthrough? Tweet it. Just had a great lesson? Tweet it. Just had a eureka moment? Tweet it. You'll end up in a network of teachers doing the same. It becomes an easy way to collaborate, to share, and to promote all the great stuff you're already doing.

5. **Put Yourself on the School Board Meeting Agenda**—Make the board meeting an open mike night for teacher successes. Imag-

ine if there were a line of teachers on the agenda to pass the mike to.

6. **Adopt a Bulletin Board**—Sign up to provide the content for the hallway bulletin board for some of your students' best work. Include a description of the lesson, photos, and quotes. Let the students design the board. After all, you're busy, and they are willing, proud, and eager to create a bulletin board.

7. **Wear Your Flair**—There are many ways to promote our well-earned credentials. Doctors hang their degrees in a wooden frame. So why can't we advertise our own degrees and professional communities?

Look, teachers have been playing by the modest rules that society has long since dropped, so it's time we put on our pins, hung our certifications, and did a little bragging ourselves. Are you a member of National Council of Teachers of English, a fellow of the Writing Project, an Apple Distinguished Educator, a member of The Teacher Leaders Network, or a graduate of Google Academy? Are you a Teacher of the Year, a Nationa Board Certified Teacher, a grant recipient, or do you even have a heartfelt letter from a student to display that awards you their highest praise—that of being their favorite teacher? Flaunt your credentials.

We've invested in ourselves, in our country, and in the future of its children by investing in our own professional development and lifelong learning. Some teachers have more education than lawyers or doctors, yet we are treated like assembly-line workers. Why? Because we don't demand otherwise. And publicity is the key to getting our voices out there. So wear your flair.

This isn't just about showing off; it's about pitching what works so that your programs are funded. It's about pitching your accomplishments so that people better appreciate our profession. It's about pitching the talents of the students and the staff so that enrollment doesn't drop from elementary to middle school. You don't have to start with calling a newspaper. It all begins with calling an extension on your own school site.

You can't rely on principals to know that cool stuff is happening; you have to call them in when it is. Allowing access to your classroom is a form of publicity. Therefore, don't just wait for those rare observation days. Call your administrator anytime something cool's going on. Principals respond to the "Come, check this out!" call, and even if they can't come, they then know when success is happening. It's a version of transparent teaching. It's a form of easy publicity. And it's called *teaching with your door open*.

Teaching with Your Door Open

I mean this literally and philosophically. Call administrators in or give them the go-ahead to wander through anytime. Allow visitors to come in, ask questions, and interact. It's the isolated teacher that causes administrators to worry about the quality of what's going on behind closed doors, not the teacher comfortable with walk-ins and informal observations.

Besides, if you invite administrators in when you know great stuff is going on, they will be more likely to trust what's happening in the classroom at other times, and might be more hands off, allowing you more autonomy, and thereby possibly upping your happiness in the day-to-day job.

Teaching with your door open creates a reputation for yourself as teacher comfortable with her own practice, but it also helps in student achievement too. Believe it or not, if you teach with transparency, you'll be encouraging better classroom management—one based on student pride in the accomplishments of their class. You'll be modeling a comfort in your own formal and informal evaluations that can serve as a model for your students, which, in turn, helps them have comfort in their own assessments and evaluations.

Think of it this way: Ever see your students after school or on the weekends at the local market, earbuds in their ears, closing themselves off from the outside world? Well, by closing your classroom door and disallowing people to enter, walk through, hang out, and observe, you are modeling this very isolated existence.

For instance, every third period, I have a new teacher who spends her prep time in my classroom, hanging out, learning, quietly asking kids questions. Whenever visitors are on campus, my principal calls me to ask if they can come in and have these guests see whatever I'm doing. Is it always a great, stupendous lesson? No. But because my students are used to having adults in the classroom, there is this really amazing symptom that takes over any crazy urge they may have to act up: pride.

Tweens love to show off, and they love an audience. Frankly, even your most difficult of students might surprise you if allowing visitors into your classroom has been a part of the classroom culture from the get-go. I can remember many occasions when, upon seeing my lowest ranked student asked a question by a guest, I needlessly winced inside, only to discover that they had been eager to share. For many of the kids who are challenging in a classroom, talking to a visitor, one who doesn't know that student's past, and answering questions can be refreshing for them. However, you have to specifically prepare your class and classroom for visitors so that it doesn't make you sweat every time the door opens:

1. Make sure the kids have been briefed on how to talk to guests, how to answer their questions honestly but with good content knowledge. Role playing early in the year is a great way to model how to communicate with onlookers.

2. When displaying student work, make sure there are written explanations posted on the wall that describe the steps that went into creating what a visitor might be looking at. This can help cue students if they freeze. Sometimes the work doesn't speak for itself; we have to spell it out for visitors.

3. Practice transitions frequently: how to get out the notebooks with little time wasted, how to distribute supplies, etc.

4. Be straight up with your students about what you know about the visitors: Who they are, where they are from, when they are coming, etc.

5. Be honest with your praise. Let your students know that it is because of your teamwork as students and teacher that you seem to always have guests about. This is, after all, a compliment. It is their great reputation that lures guests to your room.

By being open with your teaching practice and classroom control, you make yourself a part of the dependable corps of teachers on a campus. By teaching with your door open you become a fixture in the school culture. This aids in making you indispensable and appreciated, and that translates to your greater happiness in a profession that grapples for respect. All it takes is just a little purposeful publicity on your part.

You bring students back from the brink of failure every day. You help kids learn how to think, how to share, how to disagree. You are the one who teaches them the rules of the game. You are the one who teaches them how to create their own game. You teach them how to communicate: analytically, persuasively, and responsively. You are the one who answers questions. You are the one who teaches them to question. So it's up to you to get it out there. It's not just for you, the individual teacher, but also for the good of your staff, and even the profession. Learn to use publicity so it doesn't use us all.

15

Tips for Taking Care of Yourself

...the work is finished some day, the education never.

— Alexandre Dumas

You know what presidents look like after their term in office is over? More gray hairs on the top, and more frown lines around the mouth. The pressures of the job age a president. And the pressures of teaching age us, too. After all, just because you like your job doesn't mean it doesn't take its toll on you. You have to be proactive about keeping your sanity and your health or you'll lose both.

We have to be proactive as individuals to fight the wear and tear that years in this job can have on us. Seriously, even if you come from a big family, how many adults have really spent 8 hours a day for 180 days a year with a school full of tweens? Only the educators. An adult is just not built to spend so much time with so many kids so intensely with so much pressure, care, laughter, tears, anger, and happiness. The drama alone of just being around tweens can suck the life out of the most energetic of our teacher troops.

There's a quote I once heard in a professional development seminar that really ticked me off: "A good teacher is like a candle—it consumes itself to light the way for others." I think that's crazy. For if we consume ourselves in self-sacrifice, we not only lose ourselves, we lose our students. The most powerful tool for tween achievement is a happy, healthy, and dedicated teacher.

> *You are the one in the classroom from whom students sometimes need to pull their energy, so make sure that there's energy from you to pull.*

Consequently, you have to take care of yourself. Pushing yourself until you break won't help anyone. You have to educate yourself in what relaxes you. You have to discover what excites you. You have to identify what helps you be better as a teacher so that when you return to the classroom in September, or after a personal day, or on a Monday, you are not hung over from the difficulties of life. You are the one in the classroom from whom students sometimes need to pull their energy, so make sure that there's energy from you to pull.

To do this, you need to take care of yourself both in school and out of school. For this reason, I end this book with some advice on how to do both. This chapter discusses these topics:

♦ Taking care of yourself during the school year

♦ Keeping your brain fit over summer vacation

It takes a lot out of an adult to have their antennae up so high, so often, so consistently, and you can't just wait until vacation to lick your wounds and regain your strength. However, you have to find a way to recharge your batteries even while in battle. In fact, staying healthy and happy is as much about how you conduct yourself while at work, as it is what you do for yourself outside of the job.

Taking Care of Yourself During the School Year

Taking care of yourself during the school year is about making sure you are at your best as a teacher, and some of that is about protecting your time and energy.

Make yourself a promise that you won't do things at work that will have you berating yourself later. Guilt and disappointment in how you handle things professionally will totally corrupt your efforts to be at your best as a teacher, and no one can make good decisions if they are at their breaking point. Be honest with yourself about what you need, and seek it out for the good of yourself and your students.

Try to follow these few rules:

1. When you have questions about your content, ask your department head if there are funds so that you can observe other teachers. Seek out ideas and a little content learning for yourself.

2. When the pressures of lesson design and student engagement are overwhelming, collaborate with other teachers and take some of that pressure off of yourself. You don't have to do it all yourself. Don't reinvent the wheel, especially if the teacher next door is already rolling.

3. And if there isn't anyone on your site who can help, go online and find a Ning (custom social network) or group to join that can give you what you need.

   A great example of an incredibly successful Ning is Jim Burke's English Companion Ning at http://englishcompanion. ning.com/. Burke, a teacher, author, presenter, and all-around good guy, began this online community for English teachers and it's grown into one of the most thriving cities around. There are different discussions, guest speakers, chat rooms, and shared resources going on at any time.

Another resource for any subject matter is The George Lucas Foundation's www.edutopia.org. There are discussion boards you can join on any topic, from practice to policy.

An online community that is constantly evolving yet specific to middle school teachers is www.middleweb.com. Edited by John Norton, Middleweb is a great place to go for resources about all things middle school. It was also adopted by the National Middle School Association, which has set up another incarnation of Middleweb called MiddleTalk, a discussion group for other tween teachers.

4. Find ways to keep active, even during the school day. For instance, some schools have after-school walking clubs once a week. Stretch or do yoga during your lunch or preparation time to get the oxygen back and the stiffness out. Have an iPhone? Get a five-minute exercise app to help you work out the kinks during your free moments during the day. Find moments during the day to spend time with an adult—you.

5. Spend your lunches with another adult, or just find a way to close your door. It's OK to allow yourself twenty minutes that are student free, especially if this rejuvenates you and makes you a better teacher when your door opens up again.

6. Take a personal day. It's OK. It won't kill them, and it's bound to help you.

7. Attend a conference, even if it's only for one day. Attend a professional development workshop in a field that will help your own practice. Make sure that you can come away with lessons to use immediately upon returning to the classroom as well as philosophies to mull over at a later time.

9. Sign up for an online class, webinar, or video presentation. One of the most interesting courses I ever took was an online grant-writing course through San Diego University's online extension at http://extension.ucsd.edu/. I learned a lot and use the skills all the time in pitching my own programs. Also, by taking an online class or participating in a webinar, you'll be educating yourself in the method of content delivery to come.

www.edutopia.org offers free video downloads on everything from project-based learning to brain research, and they keep archives of all their videos based on topic, so if you're interested in learning about something new, just seek it out and spend an hour with an expert.

Interested in participating in a webinar? Check out the Elluminate-sponsored LearnCentral at http://www.learncentral.org/. LearnCentral is, at this very moment, hosting webinars using Elluminate, a platform for conducting online virtual classrooms, on everything from Moodle to Nings.

Webinars and videos are great in that they allow you to participate at the level that you want: lurk and read, send in questions ahead of time, or raise your "hand" and speak. It differentiates in that you can be as attentive as time and energy allows. Once you sign up, the information and interactive experience is yours for the taking, and many of them are free.

10. Choose a weekend and jump out of a plane. OK, even though I did it, I don't recommend it. However, what I'm saying is this: Do something extreme that puts your stack of grading in perspective and allows you to return to school with a cool story to tell.

11. Right after school, go get your feet rubbed. After all, you're standing all day, and that takes a toll on a person.

Even I have to admit, however, that there's only so much you can do for yourself during the school day. You also have to use your vacation time well, efficiently, and wisely so as to return to school refreshed and ready for the tween challenges that await you with each new week, new semester, or new school year.

Keeping Your Brain Fit Over Summer Vacation: 10 Tips

Wait, did I just say "vacation?" Vacationing has become this mirage for me and many of my colleagues, something off in the distance that never seems to arrive. When given the opportunity, teachers tend to do anything but rest. Instead, perhaps they do the following:

♦ Work summer school.

♦ Attend department or curriculum meetings.

- Develop and improve curriculum that may or may not have worked over the school year.

- Build a library of new lessons because we sure as heck don't have a lot of time to do that during the school year.

- Learn new technology or new curriculum programs that have been recently prescribed.

- Continue one's own professional development.

So I did an experiment with my own summer, and mapped out my summer vacation. Figure 15.1 shows what it looks like.

Figure 15.1. My Summer Vacation

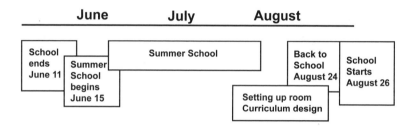

I would encourage you to do your own vacation map as well. If anything so that you can see just how vital it is to spend your time taking care of yourself. The fact is, we need the breaks we get in order to do the job that we do ten months of the year. And the other two months are spent doing other equally necessary parts of the job.

The good news is that in your off time, even as little as it is, there are ways to not only relax, but also ways to keep your brain fit. Just as students experience what I like to call "brain leakage" over their vacations, so do teachers.

For teachers, that brain leakage isn't so much lost information as a fear of the mental fatigue we know is to come when school begins. It manifests itself in those nightmares for the days leading up to the fall semester. It manifests itself in the exhaustion you feel just after two days of school. It also manifests itself in the "I'm already behind!" feeling just after those first few days, when all you may have done so far is gone over school rules and opening routines.

So before leakage occurs, what can a teacher do in their free time to maintain a certain momentum and sharpness of thought that can aid in a calmer return-to-school season? As I said earlier, the brain is a muscle, at least you can think of it as one. You have to use it to build it; the brain doesn't halt its potential just because school lets out for summer.

For the same reason a weightlifter varies his or her arm exercises to build up his or her biceps, so do teachers need to vary their brain exercises to build up their brains. And from June to August, there are great, diverse activities that you can do to keep your brain fit, resulting in an easier transition back to school.

1. **Go to Museums**—Walk, drive, or even fly to some history, science, art, or industry museum in your state. Make sure you take the audio tour, if it's available. You learn some great, little known facts on an audio tour. You also get to hear some really talented narrators or actors. Some are even full-productions with sound effects and music for some real edutainment bang.

2. **See Movies**—Rent movies you missed while grading papers. Go to movies, ranging from the blockbusters to small indie flicks. Have you ever opened up *People Magazine* and realized that there's this whole demographic of celebrities you've never seen before? Catch up on culture that flew by during the school year.

3. **Read**—Read a book that you can't find in Scholastic Book Clubs. Read old classics and new. Read employee pics and *New York Times* bestsellers. Finally, read the books for your book club that you claimed you'd read, but hadn't had time to really read. Read books recommended and some you've never heard about. Immerse yourself in literature.

   Make sure you also read the books that your students are reading. Discover different genres you may not have sampled before. Devour Manga. Get lost in gorgeous picture books. Inhale sci-fi, young adult, fantasy. Join the legions of tweens who've read about vampires. Come back to school armed to participate in the tween discussions.

4. **Go to a Botanical Garden**—Sit quietly in nature and look at everything around you. Notice architecture and landscaping. Lay in the grass. Hike to a waterfall.

5. **Garden**—Grow something that isn't someone else's kid.

6. **Volunteer**—Find a cause that you can really get behind. Find something that gives you the immediate gratification of giving. It's addictive. Build, donate, deliver, cook, whatever stimulates you. Make sure you do something for someone in need. Don't forget that in the process of building your brain, you should not neglect your heart.

7. **Do Art**—Paint, sculpt, keep a book of doodles. Recent studies show that for some people, doodling is a form of multitasking that even helps brain achievement. Try your hand at an art form

you never even conceived of doing. You know that dance studio that just opened down the street that claims it'll help you dance like a star? Try it. All you'll lose is the first free class, and you might gain a passion.

I have a colleague who decided one summer to take a correspondence class in watercolors. She gained a new interest and scored units that helped her bump along the pay scale because it addressed her need to add nonlinguistic elements into her curriculum. She also gained a one-of-a-kind watercolor for her bathroom wall.

8. **Be Active**—Run, walk, hike, jog, garden, swim. Remember that getting more oxygen to the brain increases its productivity. You will be able to do more, think quicker, and build more brain muscle when you deliver more oxygen to fuel your cranium workouts. Being stagnant can cause depression and might make you see upcoming challenges out of whack. Remember that when you're blue or bored or angry, movement will help bring more color to your life, level out your anger, and release your boredom. As a teacher, it's hard to keep the challenges in perspective. Being active all year long will help you look at things clearer.

9. **Rest**—That's right. After you've moved and worked and painted and observed, make sure that you just lay right down and rest. Sigh.

10. **Don't Just Review, Learn Something New**—I think this is the most important step of them all. You'll notice that most of these steps boil down to this one simple thought: keep learning. Take classes. Maintain your professional development. Be a student. Learning begets the desire to keep learning. It's addictive. Your brain will thank you.

I'm lucky enough to have grown up with a family that cheered when someone came home with something newly learned. Hanging in my living room was a calligraphic quote from T.H. White's *The Once and Future King* (New York: Collins, 1958). I want to share it with you now as you contemplate your own life-long learning:

> *Learning begets the desire to keep learning. It's addictive.*

"The best thing for being sad," replied Merlin, beginning to puff and blow, "is to learn something....You may grow old and trembling in your anatomies,...you may miss your only love, you may see the world about you devastated by evil lunatics, or know your honour trampled in the sewers of baser minds. There is only one thing for it then—to learn. Learn why the world wags and what wags it. That is the only thing which the mind can never exhaust, never alienate, never be tortured by, never fear or distrust, and never dream of regretting. Learning is the only thing for you."

And for many brave souls out there, teaching tweens is the only thing for us.

We are the tween teachers, "we few, we happy few, we band of brothers," who can see the potential in students even in their most invisible time of life. We pick up broken hearts, bruised for the first time, with our teachings. We see mistakes over and over, yet forgive so that the ever-evolving tween can have the chance to define themselves once more. We are here to help bridge the chasm between childhood and adulthood.

We are the tween teachers who may share a bit of the insanity with our clientele, but who also share our wisdom and passion for our content at one of the last impressionable stages of a student's life.

We are the tween teachers, brave, vital, a little off our rockers, yes, but an important variable in our children's success.

Bibliography

Anderson, J. (2005). *Mechanically inclined*. Portland, ME: Stenhouse.

Atwell, N. (1998). *In the middle: New understandings about writing, reading, and learning*. Portsmouth, NH: Heinemann.

AVID. (2010). *Costas levels of questioning*. Retrieved from http://www.avid.org/dl/eve_natcon/natcon_2009_stusuccesshandouts.pdf.

America's Choice. (2010). http://www.americaschoice.org/.

Aristotle. (2004). *Gifted and gone: Proverbs, quotations, sayings and more* (Giles, Carol, Ed.). Lincoln, NE: iUniverse.

Blau, S. (2007, June). *Proceedings of The University of California Irvine Writing Project*. Irvine, CA.

Brandeis, L. D. (1999). *Brandeis on Zionism: A collection of addresses and statements by Louis D. Brandeis*. Union, NJ: Lawbook Exchange.

California Department of Education. (2009). The California Standards for Teaching. Retrieved from http://www.ctc.ca.gov/educator-prep/standards/CSTP-2009.pdf.

Cicero, M. T. (2007). *Geary's guide to the world's great aphorists* (Geary, James, Ed.). New York: Bloomsbury.

Cleveland, B. (2009, November). Elm Public Relations. Personal correspondence.

Cody, A. (2009, December). Personal correspondence.

Cohen, D. (2009, December). Personal correspondence.

Common Sense Media, Inc. (2010). http://cybersmartcurriculum.org/.

Darwin, C. (2010). *Darwin* (Brown, William and Fabian, Andrew C., Eds.). New York: Cambridge Univ. Press.

Delahanty, K. (2009, December). Personal correspondence.

Drucker, P. F. Retrieved from http://www.brainyquote.com/quotes/authors/p/peter_drucker.html.

Dumas, A. (1891). *The memoirs of Alexandre Dumas (pére)* (Davidson, A. F., Trans.). London: W. H. Allen.

Fisher, D. & Frey, N. (2008). *Word wise and content rich*. Portsmouth, HN: Heinemann.

Gallagher, K. (2006). *Teaching adolescent writers*. Portland, ME: Stenhouse.

Gardner, H. (2006). *Multiple intelligences: New horizons in theory and practice*. New York: Basic Books.

The George Lucas Educational Foundation. (2010). www.edutopia.com.

Godin, S. (2010). http://www.sethgodin.com/sg/.

Gordon, E. (2007, June). University of California Irvine, Irvine, CA.

Hughes, C. E. (1997). *The Forbes book of business quotations* (Goodman, T., Ed.). New York: Black Dog & Levanthal.

Jackson, R. R. (2009). *Never work harder than your students and other principles of great teaching*. Alexandria, VA: ASCD.

Jago, C. (2005). *Papers, papers, papers: An English teacher's survival guide*. Portsmouth, NH: Heinemann.

Jenson, E. (2005) *Teaching with the brain in mind* (rev. 2nd ed.). Alexandria, VA: ASCD.

Kawasaki, G. (1995, June 11). "Hindsights." Palo Alto High School Baccalaureate speech, Palo Alto, CA. Retrieved on July 31, 2010 from http://www.guykawasaki.com/downloads/baccalaureate.pdf.

Keivit, B. (2010, May). Personal correspondence.

Mali, T. (2010). *What teachers make*. Retrieved from www.taylormail.com.

Marzano, R. (2006). *Classroom assessment & grading that work*. Alexandria, VA: ASCD.

Mead, M. (1992). *The Utne Reader*.

Miller, D. (2009). *The book whisperer: Awakening the inner reader in every child*. San Francisco: Jossey-Bass.

Miller, D. (2010, January). Personal correspondence.

November, A. (2009). www.novemberlearning.com.

Olson, C. B. (2010). *The reading/writing connection: Strategies for teaching and learning in the secondary classroom* (3rd ed.). Boston, MA: Allyn & Bacon.

Parks, J. L. (2004). *Teacher under construction: Things I wish I'd known*. Lincoln, NE: Weekly Reader Teacher's Press.

Pew Internet and American Life Project, Pew Research Center. (2010). Retrieved on from http://www.pewinternet.org/Reports/2010/Social-Media-and-Young-Adults.aspx.

Rippa, M. (2008). *Proceedings of The University of California Irvine Writing Project*. Irvine, CA.

Robinson, K. (2010). *TED—Sir Ken Robinson: Creating conditions where kids' natural talents can flourish*. Retrieved from http://www.reidwalley.com/2010/12/12/ted-sir-ken-robinson-creating-conditions-where-kids-natural-talents-can-flourish/.

Rozema, R., & Webb, A. (2008). *Literature and the web: Reading and responding with new technologies*. Portsmouth, NH: Heinemann.

Shepherd, P. (Producer). (2002). *The teen species*. TLC and BBC.

Smith, F. (2007). *The gigantic book of teachers' wisdom* (Gruwell, Erin, Ed.). New York: Skyhorse.

Solis, B. (2008). *The social revolution is our industrial revolution*. http://www.briansolis.com/2008/07/social-revolution-is-our-industrial/.

Teacher Created Resources. http://teachercreated.com.

TED: Ideas Worth Spreading. (2010). http://www.ted.com.

ThinkExist.com. (2009). http://thinkexist.com/quotations/education/.

Wagner, J. (1986). *The search for signs of intelligent life in the universe*. New York: Harper & Row.

Wilhelm, J. (2008). *Improving comprehension with think-aloud strategies: Modeling what good readers do*. New York: Scholastic.

Willis, J. (2007). *Brain-friendly strategies for the inclusion classroom*. Alexandria, VA: ASCD.

Willis, J. (2007, November). www.radteach.com.

Willis, J. (2006). *Research-based strategies to ignite student learning: Insights from a neurologist and classroom teacher*. Alexandria, VA: ASCD.

Wormeli, R. (2001). *Meet me in the middle*. Portland, ME: Stenhouse.